Haunted Michigan
Recent Encounters with
Active Spirits

Rev. Gerald S. Hunter

THUNDER BAY
—— P R E S S ——

West Branch, Michigan

Haunted Michigan:
Recent Encounters with Active Spirits
by Rev. Gerald S. Hunter

Copyright © 2000 by Gerald S. Hunter

Originally Published October 2000
Lake Claremont Press
Chicago, IL 60625

Published October 2006
Thunder Bay Press
Holt, Michigan 48842

First Thunder Bay Press printing, 2006

ISBN 10: 1-933272-00-7
ISBN 13: 978-1-933272-00-9

Printed in the United States of America

Contents

Foreword

What you are about to encounter is a collection of stories—ghost stories, to be exact. Between the covers of *Haunted Michigan* you will meet all sorts of lively spirits. There are young ghosts and old ghosts, male ghosts and female ghosts, nice ghosts and not-so-nice ghosts. What makes this book unique is the fact that each chapter recounts an actual haunting.

As you peruse these pages, you will quickly discover that these are not ancient ghost stories, or legendary accounts of spooky events of long ago. Instead, these are modern ghost stories, stories I guarantee you've never heard or read about before. These hauntings are active. That is to say, they continue to this day.

No doubt some of you have noticed the title "Rev." attached to my name on the cover of this book. That will lead some of you to wonder how the belief in the existence of ghosts meshes with an expression of religious faith. Let me simply say that nothing within these pages attempts to connect the two. I am simply relating to you what I have heard, what I have experienced, and what I have investigated. It is not up to me to convince you of the validity of the hauntings. Read what I have written and make up your own mind. As for myself, I am satisfied in my belief that death does not put an end to human existence. That being the case, why is it not possible that for some reason some folks continue to hang around long after the date of their mortal demise?

How does a man of my stature explain such an involvement in the macabre? It's all quite simple, actually: I grew up in a haunted house. Encountering spirits and finding yourself privy to their shenanigans on an almost daily basis for several years tends to open one's mind to the possibility that we are not always alone within the confines of our happy homes. One comes to believe that our world is both material and ethereal, a mysterious blend of objective reality and subjective experience.

Some of you may be asking how it is I've come to accumulate such an expanded repertoire of tingling tales. My answer is that I've come by them honestly. The fact that there are so many of them is due to that common phenomenon, "the snowball effect." Take a snowball and roll it down a hill. As it tumbles along, it picks up more and more snow until it is much larger at the bottom of the hill than it was at the top. That has been my experience with these stories. When people discover I investigate hauntings as a hobby, they feel free to open up about experiences they have had, or experiences friends and relatives have had. I simply follow their leads, check out their stories, and, if they have substantial merit, add them to my collection.

It's amazing how many rational, productive adults get their jollies out of reading ghost stories and in turn having the living pejeebers scared out of them. I've taken an odd delight in haunted-house lore since I've been old enough to read. However, I've grown weary of mere legends, and the ghostly experiences of 100, 50, or even 25 years ago no longer pack the paranormal punch required to tickle my terror bone. Sensing that others must share this frustration, I've decided to go public with my collection of "newly" haunted places. Because it has been my wish to substantiate each story and investigate each location personally, I've limited my research to my home state of Michigan.

It is possible for you to visit some of these haunted structures, but I've found it necessary to blur the locations of others. Because some folks treasure their anonymity, I've tinkered with addresses and taken literary license with proper names. This in no way affects the truth of these tales. These spirits exist. The places mentioned herein may well be near your neighborhood or within driving distance of your home town.

I believe certain pleasures in life are to be savored. One is ill-advised to gulp down a fine wine or gluttonously attack a gourmet meal. So it is with ghost stories. Reading them is an art form and requires a little finesse. There must be a method to being driven mad. So, be patient and wait until the shadows of night have cast a pall over the serenity of your peaceful abode. Then, snuggle into your favorite overstuffed chair, pour yourself a bracing bolt of 80-proof courage, and open your mind to the presence of the paranormal which surrounds us all.

Now, go forth, dear reader, and enjoy these true stories of current hauntings, confined within the borders of the two panoramic peninsulas so many of us lovingly refer to as Michigan.

The Haunt Meter

While polishing off the remnants of my manuscript, I thought it would be fun to offer the reader some idea of the effect each story had on me during the course of my investigations. Hence, I am sharing what I have affectionately dubbed the "Haunt Meter," a system which rates each haunted place according to the level of its scare quotient and frequency of paranormal activity.

The Haunt Meter simply uses the familiar system of ranking by stars. The higher the frights, the higher the rating. Since many of the stories I investigated turned out to be pure hokum, rating a mere one or two stars, they died an early death, falling victim to the dreaded "delete" key on my computer. I've included only those chapters that I believe to be both genuine, and genuinely frightening.

So, here it is, for the first time in print, Rev. Gerry's official Haunt Meter!

*

*A pretty lame haunting,
not worthy of my efforts or your time.*

* *

The ghosts are there, but the scares aren't.

* * *

A good haunting—some chills and goose bumps.

* * * *

*Don't enter these places alone!
Eerie and lots of activity.*

* * * * *

*Watch your backside!
Macabre and downright frightening.*

Haunted Michigan

Night Lights

Place Visited: A brick ranch home, circa 1960, one mile north of Adrian on M-52

Period of Haunting: Summer, 1992

Date of Investigation: Summer, 1992

Description of Location: Adrian is a busy and culturally-mixed city located in the midst of Lenawee County in southeastern Michigan. It is home to Adrian College, a school affiliated with the United Methodist Church; Merillat Industries, a nationally-known cabinet manufacturer; and Croswell Opera House, believed to be the oldest continuously-operating opera house in Michigan. Among the larger employers in the area are General Motors and Bixby Hospital. Adrian is located about 30 miles northwest of Toledo and about 40 miles southwest of Detroit. If traversing either the I-94 or US-12 corridors, exit at M-52 and head south.

The Haunt Meter: * * * *

Tom arrived home well after midnight on a humid mid-July night. Exhausted from his nine-hour shift at the Ford plant in nearby Saline, he crept down the stairway and into the basement where he could welcome its cool dampness upon his sweaty skin. A good night's rest in the makeshift basement bedroom would be just what the doctor ordered on yet another stifling summer's night.

Tom and Eve had moved into their new home a mere

one month earlier. Both worked for the Ford Motor Company as hourly employees—Tom on the afternoon shift and Eve on midnights. They enjoyed the spacious yard and the fact that they were no longer hemmed in by rows and rows of homes as in their previous subdivision. With their three children grown and moved away, and two incomes to make life a bit easier, they were pleased to find themselves able to afford such a spacious home.

The sprawling brick ranch sported a well-manicured lawn and a wide concrete driveway. Inside were three large bedrooms, a kitchen, a huge living room, two baths, and a dining room they had converted into a curio room for Eve's ceramic collection. A full basement included a laundry area, a workout room, a small kitchen, and a woodshop where Tom could busy himself with his hobby of furniture restoration.

It wasn't uncommon for Tom to sleep in the basement on hot summer nights. Though the home was air-conditioned, he couldn't see running up the electric bill to keep cool when all he had to do was stretch out on the cot he had set up against the back wall. So, without bothering to even wash the smell of machine oil from his hands, he stripped down to his undershorts and rested his weary muscles on the sheeted mattress.

Tom hadn't been prone on his cot for more than a few seconds when the fluorescent light on the stove nearby began to softly glow white, and then turn itself on. More tired than puzzled, he strode over to the stove and switched the light back off. Then, returning to his cot, he once again rested his body across the mattress. Within an instant, the light once again began to shimmer, and soon the bulb bathed the stove in its fluorescent glow. Tom is a no-nonsense man, well over six feet and still well-proportioned after nearly 25 years on the assembly line. Still, this was getting to feel a bit strange. He knew he had switched the light off and that it could only be turned on by manually pushing the light's toggle switch to the "on" position. So, once again he raised himself from his cot and switched off the light. This time, he never even made it back to the cot before he heard the switch click and saw the glow of the light once more splitting across the blackness of the basement.

It was then that Tom noticed just how cold his surroundings had become. "I actually began to shiver it was so freezing down there," remembers Tom. "Even in just the glow of the stove's fluorescent light, I could see my breath. That's when I jumped back onto my cot— only this time I'm sort of embarrassed to say I pulled the sheets up over my head and started praying. I knew something was down there with me, and I didn't know what or who it was."

While lying there praying and shaking from both cold and fear, Tom suddenly felt the palm of a hand gently press down upon his chest. When his natural instincts led him to resist, the hand began to push down more and more forcefully, as if someone were trying to prevent him from raising himself up off of the cot. "It lasted about a minute," says Tom, "and then it slowly and gently lifted off my chest. I remember there was no way I wanted to stay down in that basement, but there was no way I could find enough courage to make myself run upstairs. So eventually, the coldness went away, and somehow I managed to drift off to sleep."

That next weekend, Tom related to Eve what he had experienced in their basement. That's when Eve began to admit to her husband that she had to force herself to go downstairs to do the laundry. Sometimes, she said, she could detect the distinct scent of a woman's cologne, while at other times the air seemed filled with the acrid stench of rotting meat.

Several months passed before the next apparitional experience. Tom had gone down to his woodshop to finish a cradle he was working on as a gift for his expectant daughter.

I'd been down there at least an hour or so, totally

immersed in what I was doing, which was applying lacquer to the cradle. I all of a sudden got the urge to look up, and over to the far corner of the basement, where the sump pump was, there stood a woman, just as solid as if it were my wife standing there. She stood there perfectly motionless, her arms down at her sides and her head slightly tilted to her left. She was dressed in modern-looking clothes—dress slacks and a sweater. I thought for a minute that maybe I'd inhaled too many lacquer fumes, but I watched her for about two or three minutes. She never moved or even seemed to notice me. I remember I couldn't see her feet, that they seemed to be down inside the sump pump hole a little ways. She couldn't have been any more than 25 feet away from me. Then I looked down for a second, and when I looked back up she was gone.

The cold, the flashing lights, the odd scents and the woman in the basement were enough for Tom and Eve. While they were considering the idea of calling in their pastor to bless their house, they remembered how they had bought the home as part of an estate sale. Going over to the nearest neighbor, a retired farmer who had spent his entire life across the road from their house, Tom began gathering information.

"According to this old guy," says Tom,

the lady who lived in the house before us was kind of fragile in the mind. Her marriage was shaky, and this only added to her stress. From what I was told, one day her teenage son came home from school and found his mother dead in the basement. She had taken the sash from a robe and hanged herself from the copper water pipes, just above the sump pump hole. That would seem to explain the woman I saw, and how her feet weren't visible to me. I think maybe it was her who was turning on the stove light and who held me down on the cot that night.

In further conversations with the gentleman farmer across the street, Tom discovered that they weren't the only ones to complain about the woman in the base-

ment. After the woman had hanged herself, the old
farmer had volunteered to help the rest of the family
move out, as they had no desire to live in the house
where their loved one had committed suicide. "He said
they were packing up boxes and loading them into
trucks," says Tom, "when he went down to the basement to bring up some crates. While down there, he said
he heard a woman crying off in the corner, but there
was no one there. When he mentioned it to the family,
the boy who had found his mother hanging from the
pipes said that it had to be his mother, that he had seen
her more than once down in the basement, over by the
sump pump."

Tom and Eve remained in the home another two
years before selling and moving to a home with more
room for Tom's woodworking hobby and less yard work
responsibility. He insists the haunting didn't influence
their move, but admits he doesn't miss the place very
much and wishes whomever lives there now the best of
luck.

2

Cold Baths, Lost Jewelry, and Someone Watching

Place Visited: A large, two-and-a-half story home with a full basement, located on Porter Street in Albion, Michigan

Period of Haunting: 1984-1987 (probably still haunted)

Date of Investigation: Fall, 1987

Description of Location: Albion is a college town, home to Albion College, a liberal arts school of fine reputation, known in particular for its excellent pre-med program. Albion is located in Calhoun County in south central Michigan. To get to Albion, drive west from Detroit on I-94 and through Jackson. Albion is about 15 minutes farther west. Exit the freeway at M-99. The haunted home can be found by taking Business 99 to Clark, turning left, continuing to Porter, and making a right. The house in question is just up the street. I withhold the address so as to protect the current occupant from unwelcome visitors.

The Haunt Meter: * * * * ½

Cal Kirkpatrick moved with his wife, Carole, and their three children into this spacious 1930s home near the campus of Albion College when he decided to further his education by acquiring a bachelor's degree. Because it was owned by the school, the building's rent was purposely set artificially low, making it all the more desirable to a family on a limited budget.

Almost immediately, the Kirkpatricks realized they were receiving a whole lot more for their money than they expected. "I would often take night courses," says Cal, "and would walk home after dark. I can't tell you how many times I just plain felt spooked as I approached that house on foot. Sometimes, I would see the drapes in the study partially separate, as though someone were watching me as I came down the street. When I'd get inside, everyone would be in bed."

The kids were a bit anxious about parts of the house also. "There is a huge, beautiful wooden staircase leading upstairs," relates Carole,

> and for the life of me I couldn't get the kids to go up those stairs alone. I would always have to go up with them if it were bath time or bedtime. And bath time was a particular treat. I would often draw the water, check it to make certain it wasn't too hot for our youngest child, Chad, and then go get him to clean him up. Many, many times the water would be ice cold by the time I got back to the tub. I'm telling you the truth here; there were lots of times when I was alone in the house and I would leave the bathroom door open while I bathed. I just didn't want to be closed up in that room—no way!

The other bone of contention for the kids was the basement. In one corner, there was a shower, an obvious later addition to the house. Carole continues:

> Sometimes, I would tell the kids to take their showers in the basement, because I knew they were afraid of the upstairs bathroom, but it was the same old story down there, too. The kids would run down, get wet, jump out, and head back upstairs in no time flat. They complained all the time about feeling as though someone were watching them. They weren't just making things up, either, because sometimes they'd be in tears about having to go down there to shower.

There are two particular instances which stand out in our story here. Let's allow Cal to tell the first one, and then I, your friendly spectral investigator, will tell the other:

> This happened late one night in the fall of 1986. The kids had all been in bed for a couple of hours, and Carole and I were staying up to watch some old movie on the late show. During a commercial, she asked me if I could go upstairs to our bedroom and bring down her pair of slippers, as this old place was pretty drafty.
>
> I brought back the slippers, and she set them on the couch next to her while she went to the kitchen to get some popcorn. When she came back, only one slipper was on the couch; the other was nowhere to be seen. Well, since the living room was dark, we turned on all the lights and started looking for that slipper. The search actually became ridiculous, with she and I doing such stupid things as looking under couch cushions and lifting the TV from its stand. We knew something strange had happened, but we just didn't want to admit it.
>
> Well, after looking not only in the living room, but in the dining room, the kitchen, and the study, we finally gave up and started watching TV again. This time, we left the lights on. About ten minutes later, Carole happened to look down, and there, on the floor between the couch, where we were sitting, and the television, was that slipper. It was right there in plain view—and there's no way we could have missed it in our search.

It isn't often that an author of paranormal stories gets the opportunity to experience first-hand the nature of a haunting, but such was the case for me when I visited the Kirkpatricks. Here's my story:

I had been interviewing Cal and Carole for over two hours, intrigued by their tales of the paranormal. During the interview, I noticed that Carole, a vivacious and quite attractive woman in her early 30s (but I digress), was wearing a large set of colorful earrings. They were silver, with oval turquoise stones and hanging silver bangles. Suddenly, Carole felt a tug on her ear and let out a little scream. It seems that one of the earrings was now no longer in her ear.

Since the three of us were the only ones at home, as the children were all in school, I asked them not to leave the dining room and to help me look only in that room for the migrant jewelry. We exhausted every nook and cranny in that room and caught nary a glimpse of the errant earring. Carole was decidedly frightened.

From that point we began, all working together, a room-by-room search for the earring. It was nowhere to be found, and I made what I believed to be an embarrassing suggestion that we look upstairs. Cal and Carole were not put off by my proposal in the least. As I led the way, we headed up the carved, wooden staircase. Ascending the stairs, I looked down the hallway to my left and there, in the doorway of one of the children's bedrooms, was the earring. It was simply lying on the carpet, reflecting the sunlight coming through the bedroom window.

At this point, Cal asked me if I would like to spend an hour or so alone in the house. Flattered that they would trust someone they had only met that day, I took them up on the offer, and they departed for a luncheon of pizza and beer at a place called Cascarelli's, which I later discovered has some of the best pizza in the area. But again, I digress.

I selected a comfortable place on their couch and quieted myself for a moment of meditation. After only a few minutes, I could hear, directly above me, someone walking about. It was a clear, distinct tramping about, as the bedroom above me was the only room in the house without carpeting. It was the sound of someone pacing back and forth, from where the doorway would be to the bedroom window and back again. It kept going on, over and over, back and forth. Finally, I shot up the stairs, ran left down the hallway and into the bedroom in question. All the stomping about stopped the moment I entered the room. I stood and listened for a while, but nothing greeted me but dead silence. As I headed back to the stairs, I passed by the bathroom, and the door, which had been open when I went by, was now closed. I got the distinct feeling someone was being playful with me.

Upon going back downstairs, I noticed the door to the study was just swinging shut. At that moment, part of me wanted to go outside and wait for the Kirkpatricks to return, but another part was so fascinated that I just sat on the couch and hoped the walking around would start up again, but it didn't. Though I never actually saw anything, I got the distinct impression I was being watched, that whatever or whoever was in there with me could materialize at any second if it wanted to.

The Kirkpatricks remained in the house until the college sold it, causing them to find different digs elsewhere. Up until the week of the move, ghostly activity remained in full swing, with lights going on and off by themselves, doors opening, and curtains parting at the behest of unseen hands, as if someone were peering out into the darkness. As of this date, it is not known if the current owners are privy to the paranormal activity that must still be taking place all around them.

3

Flowers in the Sink

Place Visited: A two-bedroom bungalow on Warner Street in Bay City, Michigan

Period of Haunting: 1980-1993 (judging from this account, it most likely continues)

Date of Investigation: October, 1993

Description of Location: Located on Saginaw Bay, Bay City was once a lumber industry boomtown. It is a popular location for sportsmen, especially for those fond of fishing and sailing. Many residents make their living at one of the General Motors plants in Bay City or nearby Saginaw, or at Bay Medical Center, the local hospital. It's primarily a blue-collar town, with blue-collar tastes. Warner Street, where this story finds its roots, reflects this hard-working class, sporting well-maintained, and quite humble, bungalows and ranch homes. If your stomach begins to growl in response to your endless hours of ghosthunting, speed on over to Grampa Tony's, a family-owned eatery well respected for its terrific Italian dishes.

The Haunt Meter: * * * ½

Beth loved her houseplants and tended them with great care each evening upon returning home from work. She kept her African Violets on the windowsill above her kitchen sink, where they could soak in the morning sun to nourish their purple blossoms. Yet, each morning as she entered her kitchen to prepare breakfast, she would find that those violets were no longer sitting in a neat row on her windowsill, but were instead neatly stacked inside her kitchen sink.

"I would go into the kitchen to pour myself my morning juice," says Beth, "and every plant that had been on the sill the night before would now be sitting in the sink. Never was there any dirt spilled or were the clay pots so much as chipped. It was as though some-one had taken them one by one and gingerly placed them in my sink. This happened each and every morning."

Newlyweds at the time these strange incidents began, Beth and her husband Karl had been excited about the purchase of their first home. Even when activities of the paranormal began to escalate, the two of them never felt uncomfortable inside their new home. "We always felt as though someone were living with us," explains Beth, "sort of like we had a benevolent house-guest who liked to play pranks."

In the months following the purchase of their home, Beth would repeatedly hear the front doorbell ring, only to find no one at the door. This usually took place in the late afternoon or evening hours, when Karl was pulling the second shift. "The doorbell would ring," says Beth, "and I would trot over and open the door to find an empty porch. It reached a point where I would peek out the front curtains while the bell was ringing. I could see the button of the doorbell depress, and I could hear the chime, but no one was ever there."

At first, Karl would laugh at Beth's remarks about having a ghost in the house and accuse his pert young wife of having an overactive imagination. That was until the night Beth was out shopping with her mother while Karl stayed home to record some music. It seems he spent the evening being constantly interrupted by the television, which would repeatedly turn itself on and off.

"At first I figured it was just a problem with the remote control, but then the channels would change

The living room of the house on Warner Street, where an invisible guest makes frequent use of the remote control.

and the volume would go up and down," says Karl. "So after a couple of dozen instances I put the remote in another room. But the TV would still go on and off, and the channels would still change. I did not want to believe what was going on, so I started to tell myself that maybe someone was living nearby with a remote like mine and inadvertently changing my channels, but I know that's really ridiculous."

Upon relating this strange phenomenon to his wife, Beth admitted that she, too, had spent many afternoons turning off the television. Only it seemed that when it happened to her, she could often catch a glimpse of a gray shadow moving across the living-room wall. Her impression was that it was an elderly woman, though she never could quite make out exactly what it looked like.

Beth's notion that an elderly female ghost shared their abode was finally confirmed with the help of her cat, Ember. Ember got her name because of a particularly foul attitude toward any houseguest Beth or Karl would host. Ember would hiss at anyone she felt was violating her turf. It seems that one chilly autumn evening Beth was drawing water for a bath. She was alone, as Karl was pulling his usual afternoon shift. Upon filling the tub, lighting some candles, and perfuming the steaming water, Beth was about to slide into the hot bubbles when she heard Ember hissing in the living room.

Throwing on a robe, Beth crept from the bathroom and peeked through the doorway leading into the living room. There stood Ember, back arched and tail flared as she angrily hissed and stared in the direction of the kitchen. Gingerly tiptoeing across the soft shag carpeting, she found herself amazed at what was going on in the kitchen.

> Here I was standing in my bathrobe in the middle of my living room watching an old woman remove every one of the houseplants I kept on my kitchen windowsill and carefully set them one at a time inside my sink. I couldn't believe what I was seeing. My eyes kept shifting from this busy old woman to my hissing young cat. If it hadn't been for the fact that Ember was seeing her too, I would have thought I was crazy.

Beth says she and her cat watched their ghostly intruder for about three or four minutes. She was a remarkably short woman, who wore a dark blue house dress with a pattern of small white flowers. Her hair was dark gray and neatly worn in a bun. The third finger of her left hand sported a plain gold band, and a silver wristwatch adorned her outstretched arm. She would reach out, pick up a potted plant with both hands, and methodically set it inside the sink until eventually the sill was barren and the sink was full.

> It was then that I knew what was going on. After she had taken down the last plant and placed it in the sink, she stood on her tiptoes to look out the kitchen window and into the backyard. Obviously, my violets had been obstructing her view. About a minute later, Ember stopped hissing, and this lady just vanished.

It wasn't until the following summer that the events in the haunted bungalow began to make full sense to Beth. She and Karl had struck up a friendship with a middle-aged couple living directly behind them. Beth remembers:

> We were just sitting in the backyard, enjoying the warm evening and a few cold drinks, when our neighbors began to tell us about the wonderful old woman who had lived in the house before we moved in. It seems that because she lived alone and they worried about her, they had made the arrangement that each night around 11 P.M., just at the start of the evening news, they would look out their kitchen window and wait for this woman to wave to them as an indication that she was all right.

During the course of the conversation, Beth also learned that the elderly woman was well under five feet tall and had recently lost her husband. In her loneliness, she had acquired the habit of keeping the television going all day and all evening, constantly switching the channels to find something of interest. Furthermore, in her final months of life, she had become disoriented, as her mind began to slip, and would sometimes be seen standing on her own porch, ringing the bell and waiting for someone to let her into her own home.

The haunting activities continued with regularity, much to the delighted interest of Beth and the distinct contempt of her cat, right up until the day Beth and Karl moved to a new home across town. They can only assume that the new owners have already become introduced to the spectral extras included in their new mortgage.

4

The Little Girl Who Likes to Watch Television

Place Visited: A Victorian Home, circa 1885, on Center Avenue in Bay City, Michigan

Period of Haunting: Though I'm not at all certain when the haunting began, I am quite certain it continues to this day.

Date of Investigation: May, 1999

Description of Location: Located on Saginaw Bay, Bay City is a single city divided by the Saginaw River with two separate downtown areas. Traversing from one downtown to the other requires crossing one of three drawbridges, an inconvenience if you're in a hurry to get somewhere and an ore freighter or Coast Guard vessel is passing by. In its heyday, Bay City was home to the lumber industry, and it shipped vast quantities of white pine to southern sawmills. As a testament to its rough lumberjack days, the downtown area at one time sported over 50 taverns, as well as its fair share of houses of ill repute. At least one downtown business still has a trapdoor in its floor that looks down over the cold Saginaw River, through which rowdy lumbermen—pockets full of pay and heads swimming with liquor—once robbed and beaten would be summarily deposited, never, as legend tells it, to be heard from again. Today, Bay City is a beautiful town, home to such well known Michigan attractions as "The River Roar" hydroplane races, "The River of Time" Civil War re-enactment, and "The Pig Gig," an immensely popular barbecued rib contest which draws entries from all over the world. Center Avenue is one of the more historic sections of Bay City, as this is where the lumber barons constructed their fabulously ornate and spacious Victorian homes. Bay City is a little over an hour's drive northeast of Lansing and about 80 miles north of Detroit. From Detroit, take I-75 north to the Midland Street exit, then head east. Cross the Saginaw River, turning left on Washington. Go a couple of blocks north to Center Avenue and turn right. Your appreciative eyes will behold a vast presentation of magnificently-restored homes. Somewhere in that mile-long stretch is the home referred to below. If you get turned around and feel lost, ask one of the locals where St. Laurent's Candy store is. You can assuage your sweet tooth there on some of the finest homemade confections to be found in Michigan, and at least the trip will not be a complete loss.

The Haunt Meter: * * * *

Rick and Joan Hemphill (pseudonyms) had always wanted to own one of the expansive Victorian homes on this prestigious mile of avenue in Bay City. This part of Center Avenue, just east of the old downtown area, was known as the "lumber baron" section of town, the place where all the enormously rich lumber entrepreneurs of the late 1800s built their magnificent homes. Not to be outdone by the depths of one another's silk purses, each house they built was an attempt to outdo the opulence of the house previously constructed. Money was no object to these rather ostentatious individuals, and many of the homes in this area are grand beyond belief, with hand-carved walnut staircases, beveled glass, and birds-eye maple paneling, to name just a few of the extravagant expressions of their wealth.

The homes in this area are still wonderfully maintained, and many of them are featured as a part of the yearly "Victorian Home Tour" for which Bay City has become well known. In accordance with this historical pride, Rick and Joan are meticulous in the care of their fine home.

It was during their housewarming party that Rick and Joan first learned about their supposedly haunted house. "We were wrapping up the evening, and Shirley, one of our new neighbors, was helping me carry the china into the kitchen," says Joan, "when out of the blue she casually asked if we'd seen the ghost yet. I thought she was joking, but I could tell she was a little nervous about mentioning it. So I just said something like, 'not yet,' and changed the subject."

It didn't take long for Rick and Joan to suspect on their own that there indeed was something unusual about their place. For instance, Joan kept a collection of hand-blown perfume decanters on her dressing table and would regularly find several of them with their stoppers removed, as if someone had been sampling them. Often, when she would come home for lunch and the house had been empty all morning, she would discover some of her children's dolls and other assorted playthings strewn across the parlor floor.

Joan mentioned these oddities to Rick, who agreed that, yes, there was something strange going on. "Several times," says Rick, "I would get home before anyone else, and as soon as I turned the key in the front door I thought I could hear footsteps running up the staircase to the second floor, like I had surprised someone."

Rick, an attorney, and Joan, a legal secretary with another firm, both decided that, in order not to frighten their three grade-school-aged children, it was best to just keep their odd experiences to themselves. However, it wasn't long before the children began complaining about toys being removed from their rooms or the lights in their bedroom closets turning on by themselves. For several weeks Rick and Joan downplayed these incidents, offering rational explanations as only legal minds can do. These seemed to placate the children rather well, until one cold December evening a few days before Christmas, 1998.

It was one of those rare holiday nights when the family actually had nothing on its agenda. We all gathered in the living room to enjoy the lighted fireplace, some hot cocoa, and the cartoon Christmas specials on television. We were about halfway through *The Grinch Who Stole Christmas*, and Christie, our five-year-old, was sitting on my lap. I noticed she seemed a bit restless, and then she whispered to me, "Mommy, who's that little girl over there?" I looked to my left, through the arched doorway of the living room. From that vantage point you can see up the stairway as far as the first landing, where the stairs change direction and continue to ascend. Seated on the landing, dressed in a white nightgown, was a little blonde girl about five or six years old. She was sitting the way little girls sit, with her legs bent behind her, and she was smiling at us. I remember telling myself not to panic, that I couldn't upset the children, so I whispered to Christie that it was just a little girl who liked our house and loved our family, and maybe she wanted to share parts of our Christmas with us. Maybe it was because Christie was so young that she bought my explanation—thank God.

That night, according to Joan, the little girl remained on the landing until the Christmas specials were over and the television was turned off. Then she simply vanished. "I couldn't wait," says Joan, "to put the children to bed so I could tell Rick what we had seen. To my surprise, Rick said he had seen her also, this charming little blonde girl, but didn't want to draw attention to her and frighten the children."

In the weeks following Christmas, Rick and Joan would be awakened in the night by the sound of the television in the downstairs living room. Leaving their bedroom, they would peer down the curved walnut stairway and see the blonde child sitting on the landing watching television. Invariably, she would turn her head, look at them and smile, and then once again vanish. "Then," says Rick, "one of us would have to go downstairs and turn off the television. Since both of us were rather spooked, we decided the fair thing to do would be to take turns."

This home afforded me, the rare opportunity to share firsthand in another's haunting experience. Invited to spend an evening with the Hemphills in hopes of encountering firsthand their waif-like spectre, I had the pleasure of their company one spring evening in 1999.

After putting their children to bed, the three of us sat in the downstairs parlor, just off the living room, and enjoyed cups of tea spiced with haunting conversation. Thus far, all I had to go on was their adamant assertion that their home was haunted. They were believable enough and, to me, if the home wasn't haunted, it looked as though it ought to be.

We'd finished sipping our second cup of oolong when Rick offered me something more colorful to imbibe. We were well into singing the praises of single-malt scotch whisky when Joan's countenance abruptly altered. "Shhh," she whispered, "listen . . . the television is on."

Sure enough, the sounds of the television softly wafted through the living room and into the parlor. Setting our whisky glasses on their sandstone coasters, we crept to the parlor doorway and peeked up the stairway. There, once again seated upon the first landing, was a delicately-boned blonde child dressed in a white nightgown. She was seated with her legs bent behind her and was looking through the spindles of the staircase as she watched television. In a matter of seconds, she looked our way, smiled, and simply vanished.

In the weeks that followed, friends and relatives began to notice the strange doings at the Hemphills, and both Rick and Joan found it necessary to clue them in on who they might encounter perched on the stairway some enchanted evening. Some friends and relatives were intrigued, while others began to beg off when invited over for the evening.

That year I had the opportunity to get to know the Hemphills fairly well. They have assured me that their haunting continues and that all members of the family are now well acquainted with their spectral houseguest. They have no intention of leaving their home and, curiously, no intention of doing anything to make their little visitor go away. "We've come to accept her," says Joan, "and she seems happy with us."

5

The Ghost and the Cleaning Lady

Place Visited: A bowling alley, a restaurant, and a private residence all situated within Bay County, Michigan

Period of Haunting: 1985-present

Date of Investigation: Summer, 1998

Description of Location: Considering the frequency of apparitional emanations there, it would appear Bay County has its fair share of hauntings. In fact, the area has so many that I opted to pare down the number of Bay County stories to be included within these hallowed pages. I chose this one, however, due to the very nature of the haunting itself—a ghost that doesn't seem to stay put. I wish I could be more specific about the locations, but when dealing with two business owners—one reluctant to speak and the other openly hostile to my efforts—I decided it was best to be no more specific than to say that the eatery is in Bay City, the bowling alley is not in Bay City, and the private residence is in Linwood. Sorry—hostile shopkeepers and surly barkeeps diminish my resolve to defend First Amendment rights! I can tell you that Bay County is just north of Saginaw on the I-75 corridor. Bay City is just to the west of Michigan's thumb area, right on Saginaw Bay. The region hosts many wonderful summer activities and festivals and offers an array of small-town-style eateries. Don't miss The Wanigan, perhaps one of the two best delicatessens in all of Michigan, offering a scrumptious and eclectic menu, as well as a relaxing view of the Saginaw River.

The Haunt Meter: * * * * *

I don't know why so many spirits find themselves attracted to custodial engineers. Maybe it's because these folks work mainly at night when the doors of businesses are locked and the daylight employees have long since gone home to early suppers and late-night television. Maybe there's something about a smaller audience that appeals to the phantoms of the night.

Andrea is a freelance "cleaning lady," as she calls herself, and splits her evenings into hourly increments, hopping from one business to another, vacuuming floors, cleaning restrooms, and emptying trash cans along the way. Her story begins in a Bay City restaurant where she undertook her cleaning endeavors slightly after 11 P.M.

Andrea would often drag her sister or her daughter along with her to this restaurant merely for the company they provided during the lonely hours of the night. On one such occasion, she and her 12-year-old daughter were in the men's room, cleaning the stalls and wiping the sinks, when suddenly the door opened, and footsteps could be heard clicking against the tile floor behind them. As they turned to inspect the area for foreign traffic, her daughter was suddenly and rather rudely shoved up against the wall, and a loud humming sound filled the restroom. Terrified, Andrea glanced at the mirror and saw the reflection of a swirling, black mist. As quickly as it appeared, it went away, and all became quiet once again.

Andrea's daughter made the logical request to return home as soon as possible. Good mother that she is, Andrea drove her daughter home, but realized that she had to go back and finish her work. That's when she decided to stop by her sister's house and recruit her as company for the evening. To her relief, sister Janice, having always been intrigued by ghosts, consented.

The two women re-entered the restaurant in question, deciding that the best thing to do was split up the chores and get out as soon as possible. Mustering her courage, Andrea agreed to finish the restrooms, while Janice wiped clean the booths and tables. It was the sound of Janice's scream, not five minutes later, that brought Andrea racing forth from the restroom and into the dining room.

"Janice was absolutely terrified," recalls Andrea.

> She was pale and shaking all over. When I ran out to see what was going on, she started to scream again and point at the back wall of the dining room. I still can't sleep at night when I think about what we saw. That wall is covered with dark paneling, and all over the paneling were faces—faces of men and women and children—staring right at us. They weren't moving, but you could tell they were looking at us. It was terrifying. There must have been a dozen or more.

This is the point where Andrea lost her second assistant of the evening. In fact, this is when Andrea also called it quits. Literally. She quit that night and never returned. On the way home, the two sisters talked it over and thought it best not to mention the incident to anyone, for fear of ridicule.

Although Andrea had separated herself from the spectres of the restaurant, it seemed they had decided not to separate themselves from her. About two weeks after her eerie encounters, Andrea was busily engaged in cleaning a local bowling alley. Still too spooked to go anywhere alone after dark (which tends to hamper a custodian's income), she once again dragged sister Janice along. "We were emptying the trash and cleaning up the ashtrays, when one of the lanes started operating all by itself," says Andrea. "The lights came on—just on that one lane—and the pin setter began to go up and down. Then we could hear what sounded like muffled laughter, like it was coming from the far corner of the alley, where it was all dark and we couldn't see anything."

About this time, Andrea and her sister were of a common mind to whisk themselves out to the parking lot for a cigarette and a nervous breakdown. "We headed for the front entry," says Andrea,

> and there it was again, this same swirling, black, misty-like thing I'd seen in the restaurant. It sort of hovered over the entryway, and no matter how much we didn't want to be in that building, neither of us was about to go out those doors. So we stood there, holding hands and staring at this thing. It kept twisting around and moving from the floor to the ceiling. The feeling we got from it was that it was angry and hostile toward us. After a while, maybe three or four minutes, it sort of twisted itself down toward the floor and disappeared. I remember the air felt really thick in there until that thing went away.

Andrea needed the cash too much to quit yet another custodial contract, so she forced herself to return to the alley on subsequent nights, each time dragging along her sister for support. "Over the course of a couple of months," says Andrea, "we must've seen this thing three or four more times. And every once in a while we'd hear a door bang or one of the alleys would start up by itself again, always a different one. The manager claimed we were making all this up, but we weren't. I wouldn't quit this job, too, just to get attention."

Andrea eventually scratched the alley from her list of employers, not certain that the minimum wage merited putting up with all these fringe benefits. Soon, however, this spectre of public institutions made the decision to go private, spiriting itself straight through the night air to the serenity of Andrea's house.

> It was really horrible. I would be home by myself in the mornings, and this rhythmic pounding would start

on the middle of my kitchen floor. The house is close to the bay (Saginaw Bay), so there's no basement, just a crawlspace, and this pounding was coming from underneath the house. It would vibrate the kitchen floor. I'd tell my husband about it, but he just shook it all off, like I had some crazy imagination or something. My guess was that this thing had followed me from the restaurant to the bowling alley and then home.

The pounding on the floor seemed to pick up in frequency and severity over the next few weeks, always taking place only when Andrea was home alone. "I finally called my sister," she says, "who already knew what was going on. She came over, and as we sat having coffee in the kitchen, it started up again, this hard, constant pounding on the floor. We just sat and listened to it, and we could feel the vibration through our feet."

When the pounding finally ceased that particular morning, Andrea and Janice decided to go outside and peek under the house with flashlights. "We grabbed a flashlight," recalls Andrea,

and headed toward the patio doors to go outside. My husband had just replaced the old patio brick with new concrete, and the dirt around it was still fresh. As we stepped out onto the new cement, we just froze stiff. All around the new concrete were hoof prints. They circled the cement, and led up to every window on the back side of the house, like whatever it was had been trying to look inside. I've lived up here most of my life, and I know they weren't deer prints, because these were huge, and they weren't made by any four-footed animal. Whatever it was walked on two legs. That's when we really got scared, and Janice decided to call a priest in Saginaw.

The Saginaw cleric declined the invitation to investigate these strange happenings, so Andrea and Janice began to get together several times a week to pray over the disturbed home. "Sometimes," says Andrea,

the pounding would start while we were praying, and

we would just try to ignore it and pray harder. A couple of times, both Janice and I saw that same swirling black thing down the hallway by the bathroom door. This must have gone on for a couple of weeks, and then everything seemed to just quiet down. I don't know if our praying made it go away, but I still say my prayers every day.

It's been well over a year since last I heard from Andrea. It is my guess that all is quiet now, but who knows? Maybe the black, swirling mass of meanness in the end preferred hamburgers and bowling to domestic fare. I'm sure Andrea hopes so.

6

Street Spectre

Place Visited: A small, brick ranch home on Fairbanks Street in Belleville, Michigan

Period of Haunting: Summer, 1995 (it may well continue to this day)

Date of Investigation: Late July, 1995

Description of Location: Belleville is a growing city in Wayne County's Van Buren Township, only minutes east of Ann Arbor, along the I-94 corridor. A popular boating and fishing locale, Belleville Lake is near the center of town and fed by the waters of the Huron River. The spirited home is nestled within a rather cramped subdivision, where the houses generally offer no more than 1,000 square feet of living space. Take I-94 east from Ann Arbor to the Haggerty Road exit. Head north on Haggerty to Coolidge and turn left, immediately turning left again, onto Fairbanks. The new owners are less than desirous of their exact address being made public.

The Haunt Meter: * * * * *

Stacy Kendricks had just survived a protracted and rather nasty divorce. She and her two girls had been granted possession of their small brick home on Fairbanks Street, where they began the task of putting their lives back together. After a few months, Stacy met Larry, a man in his early 40s who had also just survived a traumatic divorce experience. Together, they planned to share their love and put their lives back on track.

"It was a particularly rough time for Larry," says Stacy, "as his rather lengthy marriage had come to an end, his children, now young adults, had moved away to begin lives of their own, and he found himself in the process of being reassigned to a distant town by his place of employment. All of these stresses were taking a major toll on him both physically and emotionally. In short, he was an absolute wreck, feeling fragile and vulnerable."

Whenever Larry would drop by in the evening to visit his new fiancée, Stacy would notice strange things taking place in her home after he left. "I looked forward to seeing him," recalls Stacy, "but he was always on the edge. His relocation was coming up real soon, and there was no family member to go along with him for support. I remember he would sometimes break down, and I'd worry about his giving up on life. Then, when he would leave for home, usually well after midnight, things would start to happen around the house."

Stacy relates how she would go to bed, and unable to sleep out of worry for Larry, would lie awake, thinking of ways to lend him support.

> Almost every time after he would leave, I would begin to hear movement down in my basement. It's unfinished down there, and I just used it for storage and a place to do my laundry. But it sounded like someone was down there moving things around—I could hear boxes being shoved around, and heavy footsteps slapping against the concrete floor. Whenever it would begin, I always found myself more curious than frightened. Sometimes I'd get up and go open the basement door. Invariably the noise would stop, and my cat, who I preferred to remain down there for the night, would fly up the stairs in a panic and go hide somewhere until morning. It reached a point where I couldn't even get him to go back down there, and he got so nervous he began to lose his fur.

It wasn't long before this otherworldly activity exited

the confines of its subterranean abode and began to prowl the hallway and bedrooms on the ground floor.

> Several nights after Larry would leave, or even after just talking to him on the phone, I'd go to bed and someone would enter my room. I would see a large, dark shadowy figure of a man walk into my bedroom, move past the foot of my bed, and stand between me and the bedroom window. A couple of times the light from the moon gave me a good look at him. He was tall, rather well built, with a pointed nose and deep-set eyes. He was actually quite handsome and seemed very gentle, and the sense I got of him was that he was there to give me comfort, to let me know I didn't need to worry about Larry, that everything would work out well. To be honest, I got the strong feeling it was Larry's dad, whom I didn't know, and who had died a few years earlier. He would stand by my bed for several minutes and then leave by the way he came.

After several weeks, the encounters grew more personal. Stacy relates how there were a couple of nights when she had been fast asleep, only to be awakened by the weight of someone sitting on the edge of the bed, or someone reaching down and holding her hand.

> On those occasions, I'd wake up, and there he would be, this same man I assumed to be Larry's dad, smiling down at me. Sometimes, he would squeeze my hand very gently, and I could actually feel the warmth of his touch. On at least one occasion, I could see his face clear as a bell. He was a good-looking man of about sixty, with a receding hairline and a beautiful smile. He would hold my hand as if to say "everything's going to be OK," and then he would get up and leave the room. Later, when Larry showed me pictures of his father, I became convinced it was him. It was such a beautiful and personal encounter. Even if my cat didn't like it, I felt safe with him around.

While the ghost of the house on Fairbanks Street was comforting and congenial, a terrifying encounter with another entity was soon to begin. Let's let Larry fill us in on the delightful details:

Stacy had told me about how she believed my dad was visiting her in the night. I actually thought it was great, because we could use some support, if not from this world then from the next. But soon she began telling me about another encounter she was having that was scaring the hell out of her. She says that many times, just after I would leave her house, she would watch me drive away. Then, as she began to pull her drapes shut, she would see a woman standing at the corner of her driveway. She said the lady looked human, but she had her doubts. She was dressed all in black, with a black bonnet that covered most of her face. She would just stand and stare at the house for several minutes and then leave.

Well, one night I came over for a visit and I was really depressed. My move was coming up soon, I missed my kids, and I was really ready to just give up. Stacy and I talked for a couple of hours, and I remember blaming God for all my problems and getting really angry. About that time, I remembered I'd left a gift I had bought for Stacy out in my car, so I went out to get it. It's a crowded subdivision, and my car was parked way down the street, where it begins to curve to the right. I went to the car, got the package, and started back down the street toward her house.

It was after midnight, and it had been raining most of the evening, but the rain had stopped about a half hour earlier. I remember it was very warm and muggy outside, and from where I was walking I could see way down the street, and no one was outside but me. Well, as I'm walking down the center of Fairbanks back toward Stacy's, I notice movement out of the corner of my eye. I looked over at the sidewalk to my left, and there was this woman, a large woman, walking down the sidewalk parallel to me, heading in the same direction. Right away I knew something wasn't right, because an instant earlier there was no one to be seen, but here was this woman practically right next to me. For some reason, I got the strong feeling she only had the appearance of being human, because I could plainly hear my footsteps slapping against the wet pavement, but her footsteps were perfectly silent. I picked up my pace because I wanted to get to Stacy's driveway before this woman did. As it turned out, when I headed up the drape of the driveway I had to cross right in front of her.

When I got to the sidewalk, I stopped for a second or two and looked at this woman. When I stopped, she also stopped, and stared back at me. She was dressed in a long, black cape that tied at her neck and spilled down to her ankles. The cape was hooded, so I couldn't see her hair, but I got a good look at her face. She was very plain-looking, with a round face and very dark, round eyes. She wore no makeup, and the look on her face was calm and serene. She simply stood there and stared at me, showing no emotion at all. Her arms were folded, and her hands were tucked inside her cape. At that moment I knew in my heart she was waiting for me to speak—that she wanted me to speak—and that she couldn't start the conversation. But I also knew that if I spoke I would somehow be giving myself to this woman, and I'd never be the same again. The feeling I got was that she was evil personified. So, I turned and headed up the drive and up to the side door of Stacy's house. As I waited for Stacy to unlock the door, I noticed this woman had paused at the end of the driveway and was standing there, arms folded, watching me. Just before the door opened, she turned and sort of glided down the sidewalk. Again, I heard no steps.

Larry says that after he entered the house, he immediately ran to the front window to see if the woman was yet out of sight. He caught a glimpse of her as she continued down the sidewalk past a couple of the neighbors' houses. At that point, his curiosity piqued, he decided to follow this lady, much to the dismay of Stacy, who had been watching this spectral encounter through the open living-room drapes.

"I went outside," says Larry, "not 30 seconds after

having come in, but this woman was nowhere to be seen. I followed the sidewalk in the direction she had gone, and as I did, several of the neighbors' motion-detecting porch lights came on. Yet when I had watched this lady go past a couple of the same houses, they hadn't come on at all."

After giving it a long measure of thought, Stacy developed the theory that all the hauntings were centered around Larry's feelings of desperation, that he had become vulnerable and spiritually open to the negative lady in black. "That's why," she says, "I believe Larry's dad was coming to visit me. He was trying to tell me that no matter how bad things looked now, they would turn out all right. Sure enough, after his move, and after he settled in to his new house up north, the visitations all stopped." .

There's a happy ending here, which warms the heart of the most calloused of ghost hunters. Larry and Stacy married, and Stacy sold her home on Fairbanks Street and joined her new husband in the north country of Michigan. As for me, I've examined this little corner of Belleville myself and will always wonder if others in this quaint little subdivision will someday encounter the woman in black.

7

Night Callers

Place Visited: A modest single-family dwelling not far from the campus of Ferris State University in Big Rapids, Michigan

Period of Haunting: 1998-1999 (most likely still active)

Date of Investigation: February, 2000

Description of Location: Big Rapids is a popular college town, home to Ferris State University, long known to provide quality education and especially popular with students pursuing a career in pharmaceuticals. Surrounded by gorgeous scenery, Big Rapids has perhaps the most Upper Peninsula feel of any Lower Peninsula city. Take out your map and follow 131 north to exit 139 and go east. You are now on Business 131. Take Business 131 north through Big Rapids until you reach Fuller and turn left. When you get to Hutchinson, turn right. The house is within the next few blocks.

The Haunt Meter: * * *

Although a college town, Big Rapids is a great place to live, work, and raise a family. Not too far inland from Lake Michigan, it receives its fair share of snowfall, providing residents with wintry activities such as snowmobiling, hunting, skiing, and ice fishing. Summer in Big Rapids brings its own delights as well, with rafting the area's rivers a particular local favorite.

Walter Hunnicutt (not his real name) lived on Hutchinson Street for a number of years, without so much as a smattering of paranormal pranks wafting through the confines of his cozy home. He, his wife, and their three children were always more than satisfied with their laid-back lifestyle, and Walter has never entertained a need to live anywhere other than Big Rapids.

Walter has always been a rather unassuming man, not given to pretension or hyperbole, and well-respected by all who claim him as a friend. It came then as a surprise, even to Walter, when the newly dead began visiting him in the night.

It was early autumn, 1998, when the first deceased individual decided to pay Walter a late-night call. He had gone to bed at his usual time, just after the 11 P.M. newscast. Nestled contentedly beneath his down comforter, wife Tara at his side, he had no trouble whatsoever drifting off to sleep. Sometime, well after the midnight hour had come and slipped away into the darkness of the mercurial night, Walter began to drift awake.

> I hardly ever wake up at night, so I was surprised when I just sort of slowly woke up. As I did, I was aware of a white-haired woman, who, as crazy as it sounds, seemed to be lying on her hospital bed across the bedroom from me. She was really old and wrinkled and was lying under several white sheets. I remember she was staring at me with a scared look on her face. I swear I didn't know her from Adam, but there she was, across the room looking at me.

As Walter stared back at his new roommate, he began to receive a message from her. He says:

> We seemed to be able to speak with one another with just our minds, and she communicated to me that she had just died and was wondering if it was all right to move on to the next world. She was frightened, like she didn't know what to do. As she conveyed all this to me, she also told me she was the mother of one of the guys I worked for. I felt sorry for her, she was so old and scared. I assured her it would be OK, and then she just faded away. I sat there in bed for a few minutes, and I

wasn't the least bit frightened by all this. It seemed so natural—it actually seemed peaceful, and I had a good feeling about me, the kind of feeling you get when you help someone out with something. Then, I woke up my wife and told her what had happened. Although she said she believed me, she still went straight back to sleep, so I'm not sure she took me seriously.

The next morning, Walter went to work as usual. Upon arriving, he discovered that his immediate supervisor wasn't going to be in that day, that his mother, who had resided in a nursing home in East Lansing, had passed away in the night. "When I heard the news," says Walter, "I wasn't surprised at all, because I already knew it. I told one of the guys at work about what happened, but he didn't buy it at all, so I decided to just keep it to myself."

The experience never disquieted Walter. In fact, it seemed to be the start of a spiritual high, and he felt his life becoming more peaceful and calm. Perhaps it is because of this higher spiritual awareness that Walter didn't have to wait long for another visit from the recently deceased.

Just before Christmas of 1998, I went to bed as usual, with no particular thoughts or worries on my mind. In fact, I was feeling really good with the world and was looking forward to shopping for Christmas presents with my wife. Sometime around 2 A.M., I drifted awake again, and this time there was a woman sort of hovering over my bed. She was about 70 years old, with dyed light brown hair, wearing a heavy, very modest nightgown. This time, it was someone I had seen before, and I knew instantly she was a friend of my mother's from down in Grand Rapids.

Like the first woman did, his mother's friend told Walter she had just died and that she was scared about moving on. Only this time, the communication took a different tack. As they spoke to one another with their minds, she led Walter out of his bedroom and into her house, a place he had never been before.

> I remember going with her through her back porch
> door and into her kitchen. I could see her cheap
> dinette set, the magnets on her refrigerator, and even
> the collection of ceramic chickens she kept on a shelf
> above her sink. From there we entered her living room,
> which was a long, rectangular room split in the middle
> by a staircase that led upstairs. We sort of floated up
> the stairway, and at the top were two bedrooms, one to
> the left of the staircase and one to the right. We went
> to the right, and—this is the amazing thing—we stood
> together by the side of the bed and looked down upon
> her body, lying dead beneath the covers. Again, she
> asked for assurance she was going to be all right, and
> when I told her it was OK to go, she vanished, and
> when she did, I was suddenly back in my bedroom,
> wide awake and sitting up in my bed. Once again I
> woke up my wife, and this time we jotted down the
> time and made some notes about what I told her, in
> hopes we could somehow validate the whole event.

It wasn't long before Walter got all the validation he
needed. That next morning was Saturday, and he had
promised to pay his mother a visit. Arriving at his mom's
house early enough for a breakfast of sausage gravy and
biscuits, he was still anxious about the events of the
previous night. The woman who had visited him was his
mother's next-door neighbor, yet so far his mother had
mentioned nothing out of the ordinary. Then, as breakfast became a memory and lunch began to approach,
there was a knock on his mother's back door. It was the
neighbor's oldest son. He had come over to let my
mother know that he had just found his mother dead in
her bed. He said he had tried to reach his mother by
phone that morning, and when there was no answer, he
had driven over to check on her.

> He asked us if we could come over and sit with him
> until the coroner came. So we did. And although I had
> known this lady as my mother's neighbor for several
> years, I had never been to her house. As we walked in

through the back porch door, everything was exactly as I had seen it in my encounter with her the night before. The same kitchen with the ceramic chickens, the same long living room, the same staircase, and the same bedrooms upstairs. In fact, we went up there with him to his mother's bedroom, and she was lying in bed just as I had remembered.

By now, Walter and his wife knew there was no coincidence taking place here, that he was indeed encountering, for whatever reason, the spirits of the dead. For his part, Walter was not in the least put off by the experiences. They seemed to him as natural as any other normal event in his life, except that they were so paranormal he knew he still had to keep them pretty much to himself.

The winter passed, and 1999 began without any further appearances of dead folk gathering around Walter's bedside. Although he admits he missed the visits and felt lucky to be among the privileged few who have met ghosts up close and personal, he knew he had no control over when, or even if, further encounters lay in store. Then came the fall of 1999.

It was almost a year since Walter's first conversation with a dead person. The privacy of his bedroom had remained intact until mid-October, when, awakened in the night, Walter again found himself face to face with a spirit in distress.

This time when I drifted awake, I wasn't even in my bedroom. I was in a rest home standing next to the bedside of my uncle Larry. My uncle Larry had been a hard drinker all his life and, as a result, had nearly lost his family over it. Because of his boozing and womanizing, my cousins had barely had enough money for food and clothes. He was a pretty selfish, live-for-yourself kind of guy. Now, he was old beyond his years, and his liver and kidneys were shutting down from all the alcohol. My aunt had him placed in this cheap nursing home because that was all they could afford, and she couldn't take care of him anymore. Anyway, there I stood, right next to his bed. I remember that his eyes were closed, but he was still breathing. I had the sensation he knew I was there, and that he wanted me there because he knew I had always been a spiritual sort of guy. Although he appeared to be sleeping, I leaned down and whispered to him, asking him if he wanted me to pray with him. The instant I asked that, his eyes shot open wide and his hands flew up and grabbed me and pulled me down closer to him. As soon as that happened, I was back in my bedroom, sitting up in my bed.

Because of his past experiences, Walter knew right away he had to go visit his uncle, that he was most likely near death. That evening after work, he drove down to the nursing home in Grand Rapids and found his uncle's room.

It was so strange because I knew I had been there before, even though I'd never been there in my life. No one else was in the room, and when I looked down at him, he looked just the way he had in my spiritual encounter with him. His eyes were closed and, if not for the movement of his chest, you'd have thought he was dead. I instinctively did just what I did in my vision the night before, I bent down and whispered to him, asking him if he wanted me to pray with him. The instant I said that, his eyes shot open and he pulled me down close to him. I've never seen such fear in anyone's eyes before. We prayed together, and he immediately drifted off to sleep. I drove back home and waited for a phone call from my aunt, telling me he was dead. About 11 A.M. the next morning, she did call, letting us know that Larry had died in his sleep earlier that morning.

One can only speculate as to why the recently deceased—and soon-to-be recently deceased—have begun to appear in Walter's bedroom. Is it his high level of spirituality or deep sense of psychic openness which welcomes them to his bedside? Is his bedroom a sort of doorway between this world and the next? Are these strange encounters a gift from God, newly bestowed and deserving of further nurturing? Or are they a fluke, a random set of paranormal experiences which will visit him for a while and then forever depart?

Walter has no answers. He feels as though these folks needed him at a desperate time in their lives, and that God has blessed him with being there at such holy moments. He sincerely hopes the visitations continue and says he will miss them if they come to a halt.

8

Unwanted Help

Place Visited: A popular restaurant in Brooklyn, Michigan

Period of Haunting: The haunting began with the restaurant's opening and continues to this day.

Date of Investigation: March, 2000

Description of Location: The Big Boy Restaurant is located on the corner of Wamplers Lake Road and Main Street in the village of Brooklyn. Brooklyn, located in the southern portion of Jackson County, is a small community of about 1,200 living souls, which swells in the summer months to many times that amount when vacationers swarm to the area to enjoy any one of its 52 nearby lakes. Not far to the east is Hayes State Park, and just a couple of miles to the south is Michigan International Speedway. Brooklyn is 15 miles south of Jackson and about an hour west of Detroit. From Detroit, take US-12 through Saline and Clinton and continue to M-50. Take M-50 north and, in a couple of minutes, you'll be smack dab in front of the Big Boy Restaurant.

The Haunt Meter: * * * *

Some may ask how it came to pass that this book contains two haunting stories from such a small town as Brooklyn. The answer is simple—I grew up in this town, and my familiarity with the citizenry has made me privy to local experiences. Besides, the other haunted-house story emanating from this variegated village deals with the extremely haunted house in which I lived all through my junior and senior high school years. Interestingly enough, there are at least three other haunted places within this village I could have written about, but perhaps Brooklyn should be best referred to as a vacationer's paradise, not a ghosthunter's stomping grounds.

The stories of the haunted restaurant on Main Street have come to me through at least three separate sources. As usual, and as wished by the participants, the names of these persons have been changed. After all, it is a small community, and folks there seem to know enough about one another as it is, without my further fertilizing the roots of the gossip tree.

Edna Bearsley tells me she used to be a prep cook at this buzzing little eatery. People flock to its fine fare, and her job was to open up the store and start making the salads and the soups and the desserts for the hordes of hungry diners who would grace this establishment. On many occasions, at least one unseen customer enjoyed showing up a bit before the doors actually swung open for business.

"We'd come in early," says Edna,

> me and this other girl who doesn't want her name used. We'd unlock the back door and be greeted by the smell of fresh coffee. We'd turn on the lights in the kitchen, and one of the coffee machines would already be in the process of brewing a fresh pot of coffee—and those pots aren't on a timer. Someone would have had to fill the basket with coffee, turn on the machine, and punch the "start" button. There was no explanation, but this happened several times while I worked there. I'm not a brave person, and I didn't appreciate the gesture one bit.

According to my sources, the kitchen is the primary focus of paranormal activity at the restaurant. Linda Staley, another employee who worked the early shift,

The Brooklyn Big Boy restaurant where staff members receive
such unwanted otherworldly attention as freshly-brewed
coffee before the start of an early morning shift.

supports this theory. "I'm with Edna on this one," says
Linda.

> Sometimes it felt like someone knew we were coming
> and wanted to treat us to coffee. Only it wasn't a treat,
> it really made you jumpy that early in the morning (the
> haunting, not the coffee). There were also times when
> large bowls of salad would shoot off the prep table, or
> when dishes seemed to just pick themselves up and
> toss themselves on the floor. Once, I actually saw a
> plate float straight up in the air and then go crashing
> down on the floor. This sort of thing usually happened
> either just in front of you or just behind you. It was
> like someone was purposely trying to scare you.

Along with flying saucers and floating coffee cups,
both Linda and Edna speak of seeing dark shadows
scoot across the prep room and kitchen area. "It really
freaked us out," says Edna. "We knew we were the only
ones in the restaurant, and you'd look up and see this

dark form standing in the corner. Then, as soon as you laid eyes on it, it would shoot across the room and disappear. It reached a point where we were afraid to go in the place and would take turns in the morning going through the door first."

The prep ladies aren't the only ones to be entertained by the resident ghost of this hamburger haven. George, an amiable character who pulled the night shift as janitor for a while, recalls strange goings-on when engaged in his nocturnal clean-up. He speaks of waiting until all the employees had exited the building, before drawing hot water for his mop bucket. Several times, as he would begin swabbing the tiled floors, his mop bucket would inexplicably tip itself over, spilling its contents across the dining room. "Sometimes," says George, "I'd mop for a while, and then go refill my cup with Coke. When I'd get back to my bucket, it would be on its side, with soapy water everywhere."

That's not the only shivering escapade George would have while supposedly alone in the restaurant.

> I can't tell you how many times I would hear the back door open and hear the sounds of someone walking around in the kitchen. At first, I'd go check it out to see if someone had forgotten something and had come back to the restaurant, but every time I'd step into the kitchen, the door was still locked and the noise would stop. After a while, I sort of got used to all this and if I heard someone walking around, I would just stop what I was doing and listen for a minute or two and then get back to work. I wasn't really all that scared. I enjoy that kind of stuff and sort of looked forward to it. Sometimes I'd sneak someone in to work with me and we'd both hear the footsteps and the banging around.

It's not often that hauntings reach a resolution, but sometimes a discovery is made which sheds a little light on the dark happenings around us. Such is the case here. In conversation with a couple of local gossitorians (gossip/historians), I was reminded of a farmhouse and barn that used to stand on the corner now occupied by our enchanted eatery. It's alleged that the past owner of that property had involved himself in some rather heinous crimes, and, knowing that agents from none other than the Federal Bureau of Investigation were hot on his tail, promptly departed this world at the end of a taut rope stretched from the beams of the barn. Exit one accused felon, enter one troubled ghost? Maybe. The story is substantiated by the local authorities.

If interested in visiting this Brooklyn restaurant, take a seat, browse through a menu, and enjoy some truly good food served by friendly folk. On at least two occasions I visited this establishment for a sandwich and some fries myself and attempted to strike up a conversation with a waitress and a hostess concerning their resident ghost. Both times, these youthful employees begged off. The manner in which they abruptly changed the subject leads me to believe the haunting continues. On the other hand, perhaps you'll be lucky enough to be served up a spectral side dish with your meal. If so, remember to leave a nice tip.

9

Home, Haunted Home

Place Visited: A two-story farmhouse, circa 1900, resting comfortably outside the village limits of Brooklyn, Michigan

Period of Haunting: 1965-present

Date of Investigation: 1965-present

Description of Location: Brooklyn is a pleasant and attractive village of about 1,200, tucked into the rolling scenery of what are called The Irish Hills within southern Jackson County, in south-central Michigan. If pressed for time, I-94 westbound from Detroit leads to the US-127 South exit. Take US-127 southward until reaching the M-50 (Monroe) exit and head southeast. You'll pass through the small village of Napoleon. Continue on M-50 another four miles or so, and you're in Brooklyn. However, if not in any particular hurry and you wish to enjoy some of the most charming scenery in southern Michigan, saunter along US-12, an old stagecoach route linking Detroit with Chicago, until hitting M-50, and turn north. Brooklyn is just a couple of miles up the road. The house in question is almost exactly one mile north of the only stoplight in town and rests comfortably on the west side of the road, about the third house north of Riverside Road at 9746 Brooklyn Road. Be advised that my brother Mark resides in this home and that he has been the Chief of Police for Columbia Township for several years. Before getting any ideas of cruising into the drive and interrupting his family's privacy, understand he is well acquainted with the prosecutorial procedures necessary to keep trespassing to a minimum.

Author's Note: This may be the most interesting and wonderfully haunted home in this book. I say this because this is the house our family moved into in January, 1965, when my father resigned his position as a deputy with the Wayne County Sheriff's Department and accepted the Village of Brooklyn's offer to become their Chief of Police. I was 12 years of age when we moved into this antiquated farmhouse and lived there until shortly after my eighteenth birthday. My mother still owns and resides within its spectral walls, as does my brother Mark and his family. We noticed the haunting of this home immediately upon moving in, and the frequency and intensity of the haunting seems to be gradually escalating with the passage of time. I still visit frequently and continue to have access to the paranormal activity therein. There are times when we simply can't wait to see what is going to happen next.

The Haunt Meter: * * * * *

My parents, Doug and Norma Hunter, purchased this old farmhouse in January, 1965. It was in quite a state of disrepair and light years removed from the comfort of the home we had just vacated in Garden City, Michigan. The only floor coverings were of ripped vinyl, and the wallpaper hung in billowy shards from its walls. While it did have running water and a septic field, the kitchen sink still sported a brick-red hand pump, and a "two-seater" outhouse graced the view from the kitchen window. Downstairs, in a dank and musty Michigan basement, resided a wood-and-coal furnace, the behemoth of all heaters, which gobbled up cords of wood as though they were so many toothpicks and spewed forth a smoky aroma which inundated the entire abode, clinging to drapery and clothing alike. My bedroom, if you would dare to call it a bedroom at all, had been

The vigorously-haunted Brooklyn home of Rev. Hunter's
adolescent years looks entirely benign on the outside.

originally an upstairs storage room with no access to
heat of any sort. Upon initial examination of the decrepit
old structure, my brothers and I wondered aloud if Dad
had lost his mind. He hadn't. He absolutely adored the
place, happily explaining to all within earshot that it
was just like the home he grew up in back in Wisconsin.
We all speculated as to what a pitiful childhood that
must have been.

Right off, our family began to notice the house's
strange behavior. There were four of us boys sharing
bed and board under this roof: Glenn, Greg, myself
(Gerry), and Mark, listing us all in order from oldest to
youngest. Glenn and Greg were responsible for keeping
the furnace stoked during the chilly days and frigid
nights of our gray, Michigan winters. Neither of them
would venture down into the basement, which we
referred to as "Uncle Fester's Room," alone. Both complained of hearing strange noises and feeling as though
someone were hovering over them as they fed the fur-

nace its nightly snack of blackened bitumen.

One night, when teenaged Glenn was home alone and found it necessary to tread the creaky staircase down to the furnace room, he was relieved to hear my mother calling him, an indication she and my father had returned home from visiting my grandmother back east in the civilized suburbs. Thrilled at the sound of her voice repeatedly beckoning him back upstairs, he raced up the steps and into the kitchen only to encounter a dark and empty house. He never again went down those stairs alone.

My father, a handsome and strong-willed man, pooh-poohed our complaints that strange things were emanating from within his hallowed home. Every time we'd lie in bed and hear whisperings in the dark, or the front porch door would inexplicably open and shut by itself, as it often did, he would pass it off as figments of our youthful imaginations. As for us, we were quite certain our imaginations weren't turning our bedroom door-knobs as we cowered under the sheets waiting for the blessed protection of sleep.

Whether we grew sullenly accustomed to the strangeness of our rural home, or if the noise and general rowdiness of four boys blanketed the paranormal pranks, the next few years were relatively calm. It wasn't until we three oldest boys had grown up and moved out that the haunting experiences appeared to drift back into the limelight once again.

It was an unseasonably warm October evening in the late 1970s, when Mark, then a freshman in high school, unwittingly played host at a haunted card party. He had invited four friends, two guys and two girls, over to the house for an evening of euchre and music. They ascended the stairway to his bedroom, unfolded a rickety old card table, and started shuffling away. One young girl named Jill sat out the game and was in charge of music. "I was thumbing though magazines and changing the records," relates Jill, when I glanced over toward the table where they were playing cards. Behind them was Mark's dresser, with a huge, round mirror. When I looked into the mirror, I should have been able to see the reflection of four people seated at the card table. But just behind Mark was the reflection of this old man, who was just standing there staring at me. I totally freaked out, screaming all the way down the stairs, through the kitchen, and out into the yard. Mark's mom finally had to take me home, because there was no way I was going back up there.

Over the course of the next few years, the haunting continued, with whispering voices drifting from room to room, lights switching themselves on and off, and the occasional dark, shadowy form scooting across the rooms. Interestingly enough, no one actually took offense at these oddities, as living with spirits can actually begin to feel normal after a while. It wasn't until after the death of our father, when my brother, Mark, and his family moved in with my mother, that everyone decided to pay particular attention to the strange incidents which permeated the house from top to bottom. It appears the more we paid attention, the more the haunting escalated.

By the mid-1990s, Mark and his wife, Edie, had taken up residence in the bedroom upstairs over the kitchen, while sons Doug and Ben acquired bedrooms of their own across the hall. "I get up for work early," says Edie,

so I slip downstairs to the bathroom for my shower about 5:30. I never turn on the lights in the hallway or down the staircase because I don't want to wake anyone. One morning, I went down and showered, and then started back up the stairs. Standing at about the fourth step from the top I saw a young kid in gray sweats. I thought Doug had woken up and needed to use the bathroom. I spoke his name several times, but he just stood there and never moved. Then I realized it wasn't Doug, and that I could see through this kid. All of a sudden, he disappeared. I ran up the stairs and into my bedroom and just sat at my makeup table shaking all over until Mark woke up. For several weeks after that, if I had to use the bathroom at night I would wake up Mark and make him go with me. And to this day I turn on the lights when I go downstairs—I don't care who wakes up.

In the past couple of years, Edie has continued to encounter phenomena out of the ordinary. Once, while standing by the kitchen sink in the middle of the afternoon, she glanced over at my mother, who was seated at the kitchen table intently engaged in paying her bills and balancing her checkbook. As she stared in disbelief, Edie witnessed a pencil lift up off a shelf and nearly hit Mom. "It jumped right off the shelf," says Edie, "and flew right past her head. It was so weird."

My mother, Norma, validates Edie's stories.

I remember the pencil incident and it's just like Edie said it was. And not long after that, I was helping Mark with some paperwork for his private detective agency. I had made an error on a paper, so I wadded it up and set it down on the table next to me. All of a sudden, just like it was slow motion, the wadded-up paper lifted off the table, floated through the air in front of me, and came to rest on the other side of the table. Both Mark and I saw that together.

This was not the only instance of personal spookery encountered by my mother.

I can't tell you how many times I would turn off the lights in the living room, only to go back in there and find them all on again. And the bathroom light over the sink would turn itself on, too. Then, usually in the middle of the afternoon, I would sometimes hear voices, like people having a conversation in another room. All of this happened whenever I would be home alone.

Mom's haunting experiences don't stop here. She also recalls how my brother Greg, who lives in an apartment in Brooklyn, came over one afternoon to drive her up to the casino in Mt. Pleasant. She took her purse out of the closet, set it on the bed, and then put on her coat. When she turned back to the bed to get her purse, it was gone. Both she and Greg searched the bedroom, but to no avail. They then began to check the living room and dining room and kitchen, but the purse was nowhere to be found. Distraught by the loss of her purse, Mom went back into her bedroom for another look. There, lying right in the middle of the bed where no one could have possibly overlooked it, was her purse. "Odd things like that just happen all the time," she says.

> But it never seems to upset me. In fact, sometimes it's sort of helpful, like the times I'll find my dryer opened, as though someone is helping me with the laundry. Even when the TV in my bedroom comes on by itself, I don't really get scared. In fact, only once have I ever been truly terrified in this house. That was the time I was home alone in the late morning, just a few months ago. I was standing by my dressing table in my bedroom, and I heard my bedroom door opening. I mean, I could hear the knob turning, and I could hear the door steadily creaking like it was being pulled open wide. The reason I was scared was because all the while I could hear this, I was looking straight at my door, and it wasn't moving a bit. In fact, it was already open. I felt like I had to get out of the bedroom as fast as I could, like something or someone was trying to scare me on purpose, and so I did. I went outside and sat on the deck until Mark came home for lunch.

Doug, Mark's oldest son, now a young man in high school, has strange stories of his own to convey, and does so readily. "When I was about ten," remembers Doug,

> I was upstairs in my bedroom one afternoon, and I thought I heard someone coming up the stairs. I stepped out of my bedroom and into the upstairs foyer. I watched as some older man just walked up the steps, stopped at the top, smiled at me, and then just

The stairway of the Hunters' home, haunted home, where several different ghosts have been seen ascending and descending at different times since 1965.

vanished. It didn't scare me at the time, and the way he smiled was actually kind of friendly. I mean, it was weird, but it wasn't really scary.

It's not only family members who encounter phantoms on the stairway. Once, Doug had a friend named Terrence stay the night. What no one knew at the time was that Terrence was a sleepwalker. What Terrence didn't know at the time was that he wasn't the only one who walked around that house at night. Doug relates:

It must've been about 3 A.M. when Terrence woke me up. He said he must have been sleepwalking, because he woke up standing at the top of the stairs. As he woke up, he saw this man standing on the stairs, about halfway down. He said the guy was slowly walking up toward him. That's when he ran to wake me up, because he felt like the man wasn't real, that he really didn't belong there.

Doug rather enjoys the haunting of his home.

What I'm really impressed by are the light shows we get in the living room. Lots of times I'll get up in the morning for school, and when I walk into the living room, every electronic gadget we have in there puts on a show. You'll stand there and watch while the TV, the stereo, the cable box, the VCR, and all the lights just go on and off as fast as they can. And they don't all go on and off at the same time. It's all intermittent, and it's the coolest thing you ever saw. Several times my dad and I have both stood in the doorway and watched it.

Although Doug has had unusual experiences in just about every room of the house, it is the kitchen that is, for him, the theatre of the macabre.

The kitchen is the weirdest place for me. Lots of times when I go in there, I get an overwhelming feeling of grief. One night, while I was watching a movie we rented, I went in the kitchen four or five times for snacks and stuff. Each time I walked in there, it felt like I just walked into a funeral home. The feeling I got was that lots of people were in there and they were all sad about something.

The strong sense of sadness is not all that greets folks in the kitchen. "Lots of times," says Doug,

I'll have someone touch me while I'm alone in the kitchen. I remember one evening last spring, I went into the kitchen to make a sandwich. I was standing at this little prep table we have in there, and all of a sudden someone tapped me on the shoulder. Then, I felt this hand gently drag itself across my back, like whoever it was was passing behind me. That was pretty freaky.

Doug isn't the only Hunter child sharing living space with ethereal entities. Ben, Doug's younger brother by

several years, has had his own share of ghostly
encounters. "There were lots of nights," says Mark,
"when Edie and I would lie in bed and listen to Ben
talking to someone in his bedroom across the hall.
Believe me, it's really scary to lay there and listen to
your little boy carrying on conversations with people
who you know aren't there and whom you can't see or
hear."

Ben's conversations and spectral meetings as he
grew, giving his parents the unsettling assurance that
someone was indeed sharing their son's bedroom.
"Once," says Mark,

> I was upstairs in the foyer working on the computer,
> and I could hear Ben playing in his bedroom not ten
> feet away from where I was sitting. All of a sudden his
> voice got really angry, and he started saying, "you can't
> talk to me like that!" and he started shouting at
> whoever was in there with him. When I got up to check
> on him, he told me that there were usually two people
> in his room with him whenever he was alone there.
> One person he called Mr. Hunter. We have always
> suspected this person to be my dad, who died in the
> house about 13 years ago. But the other person he
> refers to as "the mean man." He doesn't like the mean
> man, because he always stands behind a chair and
> makes fun of him. But he also says the nice man
> makes him go away. What's a little disturbing is that
> he's starting to see the mean man in other places of
> the house. A couple of weeks ago, we could hear him
> arguing with this man in the living room. That's the
> kind of stuff that gives me the willies.

As you can see, this is not a selective haunting.
Everyone in the family has had their share of strange
phenomena. "I have a son, Jacob, who lives with my
first wife down South," says Mark.

> I remember one summer when he was visiting us here
> in Michigan. Jacob was only about a year old, and we
> had put him down for a nap in one of the upstairs
> bedrooms—the one where an old girlfriend of mine had

seen a face in a mirror. When we went in to check on him, we found the window air conditioner was turned as high as it could go. It was absolutely freezing in there. We were the only ones home, and we hadn't turned it on because it wasn't a particularly hot day. But it was so cold you could almost see your breath. When we looked in the crib, Jacob was sound asleep, and one of the blankets we kept in the dresser drawer on the other side of the room was now draped across him to keep him warm. It was like there were two spirits in there, one to torment and one to protect.

That particular bedroom has always been a hotbed of apparitional activity. "Things were so active in that room," relates Mark, "that when we redecorated it and moved Ben's furniture around, he thanked us because he said the people walking around in the hall at night had been keeping him awake, and now he couldn't see into the hall."

While I spent only a scant six years living in this old farmhouse, my brother Mark literally grew up there. Naturally, this is why he can relate a plethora of paranormal stories.

When I was in junior high, I had the bedroom Ben has now. Every night, my bedroom door handle would turn back and forth, like someone was trying to get in. This would go on for hours. Dad never believed me, and so eventually I just ran a fan to cover up the noise, even in the winter. And once, when I had a friend over, we were in my room working on an art project. We had been using masking tape and decided to take a break. We shut off the lights and opened the bedroom door to go out. When we did, we heard a thud, and this roll of masking tape rolled past us and out the bedroom door and into the foyer.

Much of the haunting is current; in fact, things are busier now than they have been for years. Mark says:

I got up early for work just a few days ago and took my shower. When I walked back upstairs, it was still dark outside, and the foyer was lighted by a wisp of moonlight. I looked over and saw Ben standing in the doorway of his bedroom. I was a little irritated that he was up so early, so I asked him what he was doing, but I got no answer. Twice more I demanded to know why he was out of bed so early. When he still didn't answer, I walked over toward where he was standing. When I did, I realized it wasn't Ben, it was some other little boy I'd never seen before. He just looked at me, and then he was gone.

It's difficult to say which part of the house is most frequented by this gaggle of ghosts. When pressed to choose, everyone agrees the most haunted room in the house is the one we're currently in. However, the second-floor bedroom areas most certainly have an active life of their own. "We'll be lying in bed some nights," says Mark,

and we can listen to voices talking in the hallway. It sounds like several people all talking at the same time. You can't make out what they're saying, but you can sure hear them. And sometimes we hear music at the same time. It's not any of our music, because this stuff sounds like it belongs to another era. A couple of times, while lying there in bed, we'd hear the voices, and then the bedroom door would slowly open and shut. And several times the computer we have out there in the foyer has come on all by itself, and different programs would appear on the screen.

Mark, as I've pointed out earlier, is Chief of Police for Columbia Township in Jackson County. He also operates his own private detective agency.

I have lots of high-tech snoop equipment. One night, everyone was asleep but me. I was in bed, and I could hear the voices starting up again. So I reached over to my nightstand and picked up my night vision (night vision is an electronic scope allowing the viewer to see objects clearly in little or no light). I turned it on and began to survey the foyer and my bedroom. At the foot of my bed, I could see this red glow, which indicates the presence of someone. I set my night vision down and picked up my camera. I snapped a picture of the area where I had seen the red glow. The photo is pitch black except for a bright image in the center. It looks just like an open door. I gave the picture to my brother Greg, so none of the kids would see it and get scared.

Sometimes, the ghosts seem a bit playful. Consider the hot summer days two years ago when Mark, brother Greg, and your friendly author were put upon by our mother to redecorate her bedroom. The job entailed ripping out the plaster walls and lath, and tearing out the ceiling as well. Then, new electrical wiring was installed, and heat and air-conditioning ducts were connected to the room for the first time ever. This mission completed, drywall was hung and carpeting installed. It was long, hot, sweaty work for all three of us, and we were more than a little pleased when the end of the project drew near.

As we finished our work, Mom decided she wanted cable TV hooked up to her room, so we spliced into the cable in the basement and ran the new wire up through the bedroom floor. Greg had gone down to the basement to feed the wire through the floor, while Mark stayed up in the bedroom on the receiving end. Every time Mark would pull the wire up from the basement and over to the outlet, the wire would rudely jerk out of his hand and fly across the room. Hot, tired, and exasperated, Mark gripped the wire tightly, which is pretty tight considering he's 6'4" and weighs 260 pounds, and a veritable tug of war began, with Mark getting angrier and angrier at Greg for screwing around like this when all that everyone wanted was to finish this tedious job. His usual good nature dissolving into anger, Mark started to cuss Greg out, only to discover Greg hadn't been in the basement at all, but had been standing in the bedroom doorway amusing himself at Mark's expense and drinking a Coke. The look on Mark's face was priceless as it dawned on him that he hadn't been playing this childish game with anyone human.

As I said, sometimes the ghosts are playful. But sometimes they aren't. Once, Mark, who professes to be a handyman, descended into the bowels of the house to change the filter on the plastic water line leading from the basement to the refrigerator. Alone in the musty dankness, intent upon the task at hand, he suddenly heard the tortured scream of a young child. Racing up the stairs and into the kitchen, heart pounding and pulse racing, he sped into the living room to find all the family members contentedly seated on the couch watching television. They denied having heard any childlike screaming, so Mark descended the creaky plank steps once again to resume his work.

> I hadn't been down there two minutes when I heard clear as a bell some little child screaming like he was being tortured. I was absolutely frozen in terror for a moment, and then I ran back upstairs again to see what was going on, but again, no one else had heard anything. So, I went back down—and I was in no mood to go back down there—and it happened a third time. I went back up again, but it was the same story. I dreaded like hell having to go back down there and finish my job, and nobody would go down with me.

It matters not what time of day it is, the spirits roam at will. Often, they will be experienced by more than one person at a time. "I was in the kitchen early one morning making school lunches," relates Mark,

> and as I was packing them up, I heard a voice right behind me say "hey." I turned around and looked, but naturally no one was there. I went on packing the lunches, and this time the voice said the same thing, only much louder. I tried to ignore it, but then it happened again, only this time I also felt a hand drop onto my shoulder, and just as it did, the light over the stove came on by itself. Just as all that happened, Doug walked into the kitchen. He heard the voice and saw the light come on, too. He tried to joke it off and said something like, "well, I guess they're here," and then, as if to confirm that they really were here, the

door to the potato bin flew open.

'Tis a wild house, indeed. And this author has had his share of unnerving encounters with spectres popping through from one dimension to the other. I recall how, in the spring of 1995, I took my new bride back to Brooklyn to meet the family. We spent the day chatting until the brilliant hues of late afternoon turned into the dusky grays of evening. As a thunderstorm was playing its symphony to the setting sun, we decided to go ahead and stay the night. I tossed it over in my mind as to whether or not I should inform my wife, Tracey, about the nature of the house she was entrusting herself to, but chose to let it go. I was hoping nothing unusual would take place. I was wrong.

Everyone had gone to bed by midnight; the two of us had placed lawn furniture cushions on the floor of the dining room for a makeshift bed. We piled on the pillows, spread out the sheets, and began undressing for the night. As I stood facing the kitchen, ready to pull my shirt up over my head, I saw a man cross from one side of the kitchen to the other, and out of sight. As far as I could tell, he was about sixty, a bit on the stocky side, and balding on top. He wore blue jeans, a white T-shirt, and a pair of old work shoes. He was as solid as any human being I've ever encountered. I purposely composed myself, not wanting to alarm Tracey. Since this sort of thing fascinates me, I stepped into the kitchen to see if this guy was still hanging around. Once certain that the kitchen was empty, I headed back to the dining room, hoping against hope that she hadn't seen anything. When I looked over at her, her eyes were like saucers and her mouth was wide open. She had seen it all—the same man dressed the same way. Thank God she wasn't terrified, and I was pleased to learn this little woman was fascinated when I confessed to her all I knew about the haunting of the Hunter house.

The very next day, my brother Mark was in the kitchen getting breakfast started. I was in the dining room, sorting through my clothes, and Tracey was standing a few feet behind me. All of a sudden, we all froze in our tracks as we saw the door to the upstairs staircase start to open by itself. The knob turned, the white wood panel door swung in a slow, deliberate arc, and then raised up off the hinges and flew across the dining room, landing perfectly between the dining table and the small hide-a-bed. It was one of the most overt actions the ghosts had pulled in quite some time.

After the flying door incident, I determined it was time to do an investigation of sorts. I waited a few weeks until I could have the place to myself and drove over to "house-sit" for the night. On the way, I stopped to pick up a fresh VCR tape from the drugstore. Alone for the weekend, I set up my video camera that Friday night at the bottom of the stairs leading up to the bedrooms on the second floor. It was my hope I could record some movement on those steps, or across the foyer atop them, as this was the area where so many spirits had been seen ascending and descending, popping forth from their dimension into ours.

I turned my video camera on and crept into the living room to spend the night dozing on the couch. The next morning, I rewound the tape and stuck it in the VCR. There were no visual images anywhere to be seen. Still, I was not disappointed. Although I could not see the ghosts, I could plainly hear them. All through the tape were voices and noises. Women were heard talking in groups, and children's laughter echoed across the tape. Then, not once but twice, an elderly man could be heard taunting me. He would speak in an eerie voice, saying "hello, hello, hello," and then would repeat a nursery rhyme. After each recitation, he would begin to laugh sarcastically. Though I still get goose bumps just thinking about his voice on the tape, this wasn't the most unsettling thing to be heard. Just after the nursery rhyme, a younger man's voice hushes all the others to get their attention. Then, as they quiet down some, he gives them some instruction. He says, and I quote, "Anyone going down there (meaning down the stairway) stay to the left of whatever that thing is." Clearly, he was referring to my video camera.

Fear and fascination descended upon me that morning. Luckily, I guess, fascination prevailed, for I opted to remain another day and night alone in the house. Throughout the day, nothing unusual happened. In fact, all through the evening, there were no strange incidents to report at all. Then, some time after 1 A.M., I decided to call it a night. Since I still had the place to myself, and the couch and I hadn't agreed on what constituted a good night's sleep the night before, I pursued my slumber in my mother's bedroom, the only downstairs bedroom in the house. Turning back the sheets, I felt a bit strange, because even as a kid, I had never before slept in my parents' bedroom.

I crawled into bed, pulled the covers up over my shoulders, and reached over to the nightstand to switch off the light. The instant I switched off that lamp, all hell broke loose in that room. I literally couldn't believe what was happening to me. The bedroom door began to shake as though someone was pushing on it to get in. I could hear the doorknob rattling as though unseen hands were twisting it first one way and then the other. Then, angry footsteps began to stomp across the room at the foot of the bed. Back and forth they went, stomping more loudly each time they passed by. As if that weren't enough to engage my full attention, I could hear all the items on my mother's dresser being shoved around, like someone was sliding them around with the palms of their hands. Just as I thought I couldn't take much more of this, the pounding on the walls began—a rhythmic and aggravated reverberation which shook the entire room.

For the first time in my life, I was scared to death of being in that house. Every thought in my brain insisted I run for my life, but fear kept me so terrified I couldn't command my fingers to pull the covers over my head. I just lay there frozen in fear, and as I did, the pacing and the pounding, and the rattling of the doors, picked up in intensity. I cannot say when it all stopped. The last time I shot a nervous glance at the alarm clock, it was after 3 A.M. I drifted off to sleep from sheer exhaustion, while the noises were still going strong.

The haunting of our old homestead continues to this day, not letting up at all in its intensity or frequency. Whenever I get the opportunity, I slip over and check things out. It is my intention to someday drag an able-bodied soul over to the house with me, and do a thorough investigation, with lights, camera, and, hopefully, action. I'm quite certain the final chapter of this haunting has yet to be written.

10

Whispers of Memories

Place Visited: A single-dwelling ranch home, of wood frame construction, on Clam Lake near Traverse City, Michigan

Period of Haunting: 1996-1999

Date of Investigation: June, 1999

Description of Location: Clam Lake is an elongated body of water, connected on its east shoreline to Torch Lake. Torch Lake has the distinction of having been dubbed one of the five most beautiful lakes in the world by *National Geographic*. If motoring up the center of the State, you may take US-27 north to I-75 north and move on to Grayling. From Grayling, take M-72 west through Kalkaska, noting gorgeous pine-covered hills and clear, blue streams and lakes. Stay on M-72 until Rapid City Road, and head north. You'll pass through the quaint villages of Rapid City and Alden. Just past Alden, take CR-593 up the east shoreline of Torch Lake. Turn right on Crystal Springs Road. The house in question is on the stretch of road past Chapman Road. Don't be disappointed if you get lost or make a couple of wrong turns, as you will be traveling through some of the most beautiful scenery in Michigan. While in the area, get back on M-72 and go west to M-31, which will deposit you in Traverse City, an extremely popular tourist center with breathtaking views of Grand Traverse Bay. There's an interesting little restaurant tucked away on the downtown thoroughfare called Stone Soup that is worth the drive in and of itself.

The Haunt Meter: * * * ½

Many of the homes on Clam Lake were originally built as summer cottages, which explains the close proximity in many cases of one cottage to another. In the summer months, these cottages and homes bristle with vacationers, who flock to this north country bliss for fantastic fishing, sailing, and general respite from the downstate, big-city turmoil.

Michael and Kerrie Zinn knew they had discovered a personal paradise when they moved into their new "up-north" digs. They spent their summers putting in a yard, refurbishing docking facilities, and redecorating their new home away from home. Wanting the personal touch, they opted to furnish their abode with interesting pieces discovered at garage sales and antique shops, with a few heirlooms added to the mix for a sense of connection to their heritage. Michael says:

> We wanted things that made the place uniquely ours, so when we inherited my grandmother's antique walnut buffet, we set it up in our kitchen at the cottage. I remember seeing that piece in my grandmother's dining room when I was a kid. Grandma used to love to visit our place up north, and now that she's gone, I had something to remind me of her, something that seemed to keep our connection intact. It was a piece she had inherited from her own mother-in-law decades ago.

It was late in the summer of 1996 when the first strange incidents began to tickle the imaginations of Mike and Kerrie. "One night," remembers Kerrie,

> Mike and I had gone down to the Dockside Inn, a wonderful tavern with restaurant facilities, just down the road from us on Torch Lake. We ate our dinner out on their dock and watched the sun sink into the lake. Then we had a few drinks, chatted with some friends, and headed back home. Mike went in to take a shower, and I was in the bedroom turning down the sheets. All of a sudden, I could hear people talking at the other end of the house. I couldn't make out what they were

saying, but I could tell it was a man and a woman, and their voices seemed a bit hoarse and frail, like they were old folks. I remember I stepped closer to the bedroom door so I could hear better, and the conversation just kept going on and on. When Mike got out of the shower, I asked him if he had heard it too, but of course he hadn't with all that water running.

It wasn't long before Mike received his indoctrination into the realm of the weird. Kerrie had driven into Traverse City with a friend for lunch and shopping at the outlet center, leaving Mike to find his own style of summer relaxation.

They'd been gone about an hour, I guess, and I had been outside collecting wood for the little campfire we'd have in the evenings out in the front yard. I came in to get a sandwich and a beer, but as soon as I stepped into the living room I could hear people talking. The strongest voice was that of an old woman, and it was coming from the kitchen. It seemed really distant, and I couldn't make out what she was saying. But she would say something, and then I would hear a man's voice answer her. I wasn't scared at first, I was more fascinated, so I tiptoed to the kitchen, but just about the time I got to the doorway, it all stopped. I got a beer and sat in the living room, hoping it would start up again, but it didn't. I remembered what Kerrie had told me about hearing voices, but I didn't get scared about it until later that night, when it all kind of soaked in. I mean, it isn't natural to hear voices in your kitchen when nobody's there, but at the time it really seemed natural.

Mike and Kerrie returned to their Detroit-area home, as employment responsibilities always seem to dictate. Upon their return north the next weekend, more oddities greeted them. "We drove up the driveway," says Kerrie,

and right away I noticed that the living-room curtains were wide open. We never leave them open when we're not there, and I know I closed them before we left; it's on my checklist of things to do before we take off. We were a little concerned that maybe someone had been in the house, so we walked all around it to see if there were any signs of forced entry, but the place was still locked up just the way we had left it. When we went inside, we decided to do a check of every room, just to be sure. Everything was fine, until we got to the kitchen. We noticed that one of the drawers on Grandma's buffet was pulled wide open.

Over that particular weekend, Mike and Kerrie would several times hear the elderly voices conversing in muffled tones. Each time, they would emanate from the kitchen, and each time the kitchen was approached, the conversation would abruptly halt. "This went on Friday night and all through Saturday," says Mike,

about three or four times each day. Then, on Sunday afternoon, we came in from canoeing, and once again the same drawer to Grandma's buffet was open. That's when we figured that maybe someone was trying to get a message to us. So, we went through the drawer, and one of the things inside was this old photograph of my great-grandparents, who had lived in southern Tennessee and had passed this buffet down to my grandmother. I talked it over with Kerrie, and we thought maybe the voices were coming from my great-grandparents, and that they wanted this picture displayed somewhere. It was an ancient photo of the two of them all dressed up and was probably taken on their wedding day.

Mike and Kerrie agreed the photograph ought to adorn the top of the buffet. Kerrie recalls:

I really didn't like it very much, because I never knew these people, and antique pictures of people from another era give me the creeps. But, they were Mike's great-grandparents, and it did seem obvious we were supposed to do something with the picture, so we set it up on the buffet. After we did, all the voices coming from the kitchen just seemed to stop. To me, it's like his great-grandparents feel they're still somehow a part of the family—somehow still with us—if their picture is where family can see it. I know it sounds crazy, but that's how I've come to understand it. And I know this must be true, because I actually got to see Mike's great-grandmother for myself.

It appears that, as summer had come to a close, Mike and Kerrie made one last trip to their summer cottage before closing it up for the winter. Agian, Kerrie:

It was a beautiful weekend. We ate out at Torch Lake, visited Charlevoix's antique shops, and did some evening canoeing. All the time we were there, nothing strange happened at all, and the house felt completely comfortable. Then, when Mike was loading the car for the trip back downstate, I went into our bedroom to strip the bed. I came out with my arms full of sheets and pillowcases, and there was this old woman standing at the other end of the hall. I looked at her, and she looked at me, and then she smiled this really kind smile, and just vanished. The feeling I got was that this was Mike's great-grandmother, and she was thanking me for putting her wedding picture on the buffet. I wasn't frightened at all—it all seemed so warm and natural. I got the sense she was saying good-bye.

It is Mike and Kerrie's guess that the haunting of their lake cottage has most likely come to an end. As of this writing, the summer months approach, and only time will tell. I suppose that if they get lonely for the voices and the apparition of the old woman, they can always once again tuck the photo away in the old, walnut buffet.

11

Dead Brothers
Still Care

Place Visited: A two-story farmhouse three miles north of Escanaba, Michigan

Period of Haunting: Two appearances in August, 1992

Date of Investigation: August, 1992

Description of Location: Escanaba is one of the few larger cities in Michigan's Upper Peninsula and certainly one of its most striking. It is a port city, located on Little Bay DeNoc at the northernmost tip of Lake Michigan. From Detroit, take I-75 north to the Mackinac Bridge, then travel west on US-2 for about 2-½ hours. Escanaba is home to Mead Paper Company, a major Upper Peninsula employer, and relies heavily upon the tourist trade. The view from Ludington Park on the city's southern edge is drop-dead gorgeous. If you've the opportunity to visit Escanaba, be sure to stop at The Red Onion Pasty Shop and sample the type of hearty fare that often sustained the iron-ore miners through rugged days of underground digging. So you won't sound like a tourist, pronounce their wonderful specialty, "pass-tee." It's a succulent mix of potatoes, onions, meat, and seasonings all wrapped inside a flaky crust. If you happen to be approaching Escanaba from Wisconsin, simply steer the nose of your automobile east from Marinette for about an hour.

The Haunt Meter: * * *

Chick Hartley was going through a disagreeable divorce. In need of a place to rest his weary heart and head, he decided to move into his boyhood home for a while with his mother, Eunice. Taking respite in the home in which he had spent his formative years was seen as beneficial, and, with a few hastily-packed boxes and a suitcase or two, he moved back into the bedroom he had shared many years earlier with his older brother, Nils, a carpenter who lived in nearby Bark River.

Chick worked in restaurant management in nearby Escanaba, the only really good-sized city within an hour's drive. Summers were busy, with vacationers either headed west into Wisconsin or east toward Mackinaw Island. Escanaba is a good place to stop, with plenty of nice restaurants, beautiful motels, and Ludington Park, a gorgeous expanse of greenery affording a breathtaking view of azure Little Bay DeNoc.

It wasn't uncommon for Chick to return home late during the busy summer evenings. Knowing his mother was a bit of a worrier, he would often phone her just before locking up the eatery for the night, so she could prepare the midnight snack they always enjoyed together after calling it a day. "On this one particular night, I had phoned my mother to let her know I was getting ready to head for home," says Chick, "so I didn't think it was unusual when I noticed all the downstairs lights were on as I pulled in the drive."

Entering through the back door, Chick stepped into the kitchen, expecting to find the usual tasty meal of ham sandwiches and beer. This time, however, the kitchen table was bereft of nocturnal nourishment, and the house was quite still. "I just felt something was wrong somehow," relates Chick, "and about the time I was ready to call out to my mother, she walked into the kitchen. I could tell right away something had happened. Her eyes were all red and she seemed kind of distant."

Eunice Hartley said nothing for a moment. Then she

slowly stepped over to the sink and drew a glass of water. After taking a sip, she began to speak in a slow and certain manner. "Chick," she said, "your brother Nils is dead."

Chick felt the sharp sting of grief knife through his heart. Shocked, all he could do was question his mother. "I asked her how it happened," Chick says, "whether it was a heart attack or an accident or something, and she told me she didn't have any idea how it happened, but she knew he was dead."

Eunice could see the puzzlement all over her son's face, so she decided the best thing to do was to speak the truth. "I was in the kitchen, getting ready to fix our snack," she related to Chick, "and had just taken the sandwich meat out of the refrigerator. I turned toward the table, and there stood Nils. I knew in an instant that he was gone. We just stared at one another for a moment, then he said, 'Mom, I've got to leave now. I won't be seeing you again. I love you,' and then he was gone."

Chick was stunned.

> All we could do was sit at the kitchen table in silence, neither one of us knowing what to say. I didn't want to believe any of it, but I could tell by my mother's demeanor it must be true. About that time a car pulled into the driveway, and a Delta County Sheriff's Deputy came to the door. He told us that there had been an accident on M-35, and that my brother, Nils, had driven his pickup into the back of a flatbed semi that had stalled on the highway. He was killed instantly. From what he told us, the accident had happened about a half hour before I got home.

The next few days were understandably difficult. Even after the funeral, it was hard for Chick to believe that his brother Nils was gone. Sitting up late each night with his mother, she would remark how Nils was still with them. "She would tell me," says Chick, "that she could still sense that Nils was nearby, that spiritually he hadn't left yet and was very close to us. This seemed to bring her a bit of peace through those rough first days, although I didn't sense him being nearby at all."

About a week after the funeral, Chick and his mother were trying to get their lives back to normal. Chick returned to his job; the work at the restaurant managed to keep his mind somewhat off of his grief. "Still," says Chick, "I was really hurting inside. Nils was only 51, and he and I were close. I was pretty torn up by it all."

Returning from work late that same week, Chick and his mother shared their usual midnight snack before Chick went upstairs and climbed into bed.

> I remember just lying there thinking about how much I loved and missed my brother, and about how unfair it was that he died so suddenly, without my having a chance to say good-bye. Then, about the time I started to tremble and I thought I was going to break down, I looked over at the bedroom door and there stood Nils. He was sort of smiling at me, and then he walked over to the bed and looked down at me.

According to Chick, his brother spoke to him, but not in words.

> It was like I could hear in my mind a message from his mind. I know it sounds strange, and I can't really put it into words, but I could hear in my head every word he wanted to communicate. He said, "It's going to be all right, Chick. I'm really all right now," and then he turned, walked back toward the bedroom door, and faded away. It was like he was saying good-bye to me so that I could be at peace.

Chick eventually got on with his life and soon moved out of his mother's home and into an apartment of his own. Eunice continued on as best any mother can after a child is taken from her. To this date, no further encounters with Nils have taken place, but Chick says there are times he still strongly senses his brother's presence, especially when he is visiting his mother. "I almost feel that if I tried hard enough," says Chick, "I could will Nils back again, and that I could see him again. But as it is, I feel pretty peaceful about where he is now."

12

Some Ghosts Never Check Out

Place Visited: The Fenton Hotel, a posh eatery and fashionable watering hole in downtown Fenton, Michigan

Period of Haunting: It appears that the haunting has spanned several decades and looks forward to manifesting itself in what could be its third century.

Date of Investigation: May, 2000

Description of Location: Fenton is a lovely city of several thousand, resting just off the east side of US-23 in southern Genesee County. The Fenton Hotel was built in 1856, when the railroad made Fenton a stop along its route to Flint. It has been a successful operation since its inception, except for a brief period of time during the Depression, when just about every hostelry in rural America felt the financial pinch. After the repeal of Prohibition, the hotel blossomed once again. For many years, the original US-23 ran directly through town, making the Fenton Hotel a popular place for vacationers headed northward to dine. Shortly after World War II, the hotel gradually became more of a fine eatery and less of a hotel. And, in the mid-'50s, the hotel portion was basically shut down, and the first upper level was converted into a banquet hall. Currently, it is a rather upscale restaurant located in the city's historical section, offering such classic menu items as Duckling Confit Style, Coq Au Champignon, and Steak Diane. It is an imposing structure, rising over three stories, with the added charm of somewhat ghostly figures of yore painted upon the windowpanes of the rear portion of the building. The Fenton Hotel makes no bones about its ghosts and gives a brief run-down of its haunted reputation within the pages of its menu. When traveling from anywhere in Michigan, take US-23 to the Owen Road exit and head east. When you dead-end in downtown, turn left, and after a short, circuitous route, you'll run smack dab into the hotel itself at 302 N. Leroy Street. If you plan to visit, don't be in a hurry. Take the time to soak in the ambiance of a time long past and enjoy some of the finest dining in this part of Michigan.

The Haunt Meter: * * * * ½

Sometimes it takes great pains to uncover a good haunting story. Then there are times one gets lucky and simply falls across one. This is what happened to me when I stopped in at the Fenton Hotel on an unseasonably hot, muggy May afternoon for an iced tea. Seated in a lounge with atmosphere enough to transport the spirit to another place and time, I discovered their haunting while perusing the menu. It appears the ghosts in this establishment are so popular that their reputation has earned them a blurb on the menu right between the single-malt scotches and the imported ales, a more than appropriate setting—spirits among the spirits.

Since it was a slow Monday afternoon, I was able to strike up a courteous conversation with the owner of the Fenton Hotel, Nick Sorise, who bought the place back in 1997 after having owned and operated similar restaurants in some of the upscale suburbs of Detroit. An amiable man, proud of his dedication to fine food and sumptuous surroundings, Nick was more than happy to fill me in on the legends and lore of his establishment, as well as to guide me on a tour of his facilities.

Although resident ghosts have made themselves known to a great many people, patrons and employees alike, Nick prefers to hedge his bets when it comes to the existence of spooks in his eatery. "I like to keep an open mind," says Nick, "and even when strange things happen to me around here, I tell myself there's a logical explanation. It's how I live with it."

Although reluctant to admit belief in things paranormal, Nick is a storehouse of information.

> Last Mother's Day, we must have served 500 to 600 customers. It was one of our biggest days. One of our bartenders needed to go to the liquor storage room near the far end of the lounge to replenish the bar. She unlocked the door leading to the first room, where we keep some of the popular liquors, and proceeded through to the next door which opens up to where we keep the bulk of our supplies. As she turned around to

The Fenton Hotel (est. 1856), a posh eatery and fashionable watering hole in downtown Fenton, Michigan, makes no bones about its ghosts, offering details on its haunted reputation within the pages of its menu.

go back out, she saw this man in a top hat and black coat standing in the outer doorway, just staring at her. She said he wasn't in color, that he was all black and white, and that's how she knew right away he was a ghost. When I asked her—her name was Dawn—how she got out of the room if he was blocking the way, she told me she must have passed right through him. She was really shaken up, and shaking and crying. It took quite a while for her to calm down and get back to work.

This tale of the top-hatted intruder is merely one story in the ongoing saga of the haunting of the Fenton Hotel. The most popular ghost seems to be the fellow who holds court at his favorite spot in the lounge, table 32. Time and again waitstaff will take an order of a Jack Daniels on the rocks from a g e n t l e m a n seated there, only to discover the man gone when they return with his drink. Often, this happens when there is more than one

Table 32 of the Fenton Hotel, where time and again a phantom intruder dining solo or with flesh-and-blood humans orders a Jack Daniels, only to disappear before the server returns with his drink.

person seated at that particular table. When the server returns with everyone's drinks, she has an extra JD which no one claims to have ordered.

According to Nick, there are three main spirits in the place.

> There's one male and two females. Story has it that one of the women committed suicide upstairs by hanging herself outside one of our windows. That area isn't used for anything but storage today, and a lot of people are afraid to go in there. I have to admit the upper floors of the old hotel are pretty creepy. Even if it weren't haunted, it would make you feel like it ought to be. But the staff here really believes it is haunted. In fact, one of our girls went up to that storage area to get something, and when she walked in, she saw a bearded man outside the window looking in at her, which is pretty frightening when you consider he would have had to have been over 30 feet in the air at the time. She was so scared by it that she ran down the stairs screaming and refused to go back up there.

While interviewing Nick, I had the opportunity to take a tour of the old, historic building and check out that storage room for myself. It's a large room, and you can tell in an instant it was once used as a banquet hall. Today it's filled with extra chairs and tables and the equipment necessary for the operation of a class joint. On the same floor, there are still the empty rooms once used to house guests of the old hotel. One of those rooms, not far from Nick's upstairs office, is the room of Emery, a one-time employee of the Fenton Hotel who left this life years ago, but for some reason has elected to hang around a while.

"Emery," says Nick,

> lived here for a number of years back in the '50s and '60s. He worked here as a cook and bartender and custodian. Since we're constantly hearing footsteps walking around up here, we attribute them to Emery. In fact, sometimes after we're closed, and everyone is cleaning up downstairs and making noise, we'll hear

pounding on the walls above us, like someone would do if they're trying to sleep and you're making too much racket. We just chalk it up to Emery.

The impression I got from Nick was that he had inherited the haunting when he bought the business and that all the activity and stories are something he must endure during his tenure. I felt as though he would have been quite satisfied if the place had no reputation as a hangout for ghosts and that he only sheepishly admits to their hijinks to this day. Still, he offers up a gamut of parapsychological encounters.

> When I first bought the place, I had this really talented female entertainer who played the piano and sang. During her evening performances, she liked to drink champagne, one glass after another. Well, this one night she says to me, "Nick, I'm not singing alone tonight, I can hear an old man singing along with me." Well, I just figured she had been hittin' the sauce a bit too hard that evening, but later, during the last part of her act, I passed by and I could actually hear an old man's voice coming out of one of her speakers. It was actually mocking her. I just told myself it must have been interference from some outside electrical source or something. But it was pretty weird.

It's not only the employees and entertainers who are privy to the ghostly goings-on around the restaurant. Nick tells of a group of men who had stopped in for a drink or two and were debating about whether they should leave or stay for a couple more. A couple of the guys wanted to go, but the others were arguing with them, trying to get them to stick around a while. "All of a sudden," remembers Nick, "this old man's voice comes from out of the blue and says, 'sit your ass down.' It came right out of one of the speakers near the bandstand. I heard that with my own ears—it was so strange."

While dining in the lounge or dining rooms, customers are free to experience activity not normally associated with proper restaurant etiquette. Nick says:

> There are 250 seats in all my dining rooms, and customers from all over the restaurant will tell me they hear some strange voice calling for a man named Louie. Well, there isn't anyone named Louie who works around here. I just like to think there's a customer named Louie who comes in from time to time and someone's looking for him, but I have to admit that if there is I haven't met him.

Customers often encounter more than disembodied voices floating around the place. Often, they sit in wonderment inside the lounge, sipping their drinks as they watch the light fixtures above them swaying in the breeze, without the breeze. Sometimes, they'll even be present when glasses on the rack behind the bar decide to fly off the shelf by themselves and shatter across the floor. Recently, a male entertainer entered the kitchen during his break, just in time to see several pots and pans crash to the floor without any physical impetus.

As the oldest continuously-operated business in Genesee County, the Fenton Hotel is popular with those desirous of a classy place for their wedding reception. "We had this really nice couple hold their reception here," says Nick, "and as the evening progressed, [the bride] finally came up to me and told me that all through the night she had off and on seen her father at her reception, even though he had died several years earlier."

This woman is one among many who chance upon spirits during their visit to the hotel. One female customer, who wished to remain anonymous, was quite upset with Nick as she sat at her table trying to enjoy her meal. She complained all through her supper that some man was standing directly behind her right shoulder while she was trying to eat. It upset her so much that she announced to Nick that if the ghost wasn't going to leave, then she was—which is what she did. I guess it does upset your appetite for dessert to have a formless spirit hovering over your shoulder.

Nick purchased his eatery from a man named Gerry, who owned it for only a year. During that time, he was engaged in renovating the place and seems to have run into a bit of strange business himself. "He told me," recalls Nick,

> that as part of the renovations he and two other guys were moving some old iron heat registers from one side of the dining room to another. These were the old-fashioned kind that stood about three feet high and radiated steam heat. Well, it seems this one radiator was so heavy that they couldn't budge it, so they decided to go home and tackle the problem anew the next morning. When they came back the next morning, that very same radiator was now all the way across the room from where it had been, and there was a deep scrape in the wood floor where it had been dragged from one spot to the other.

This wasn't the only eerie event related to Nick by the previous owner.

> He also told me that just before he opened the place for business under his new ownership, he held a staff meeting to go over policies and procedures. He said that as everyone stood in the lounge listening to his spiel, the floor of the hotel suddenly dropped about a foot, causing everyone to stumble and several to fall. Then, as soon as it had fallen, it raised right back up again. Personally, I don't doubt what he tells me, but I do find it hard to believe. I mean, I checked this place out with some builders before I bought it, and the foundation is solid rock; there's no way it could have dropped. But I've talked with more than one person who was there that night and they say the floor dropped right down under their feet. You have to admit, that's a weird one.

Weirdness does seem to rule in the old Fenton Hotel. Walking through the upstairs area, one can still see the rooms where people use to lodge for the night. Although closed as a hotel in the mid-'50s, these rooms still echo with the memories of days gone by, and many of the fixtures are original to that time period. As for the third floor of the hotel, Nick balked on taking me up there, explaining that he didn't have a flashlight and that it was dark up there. He also admitted to me that it was creepy enough just to look up the stairway.

The Fenton Hotel is a wonderful old building, well-maintained and more than comfortable for its customers. A huge foyer greets guests upon entry, and there is a curved, oak front desk behind which are the individual mail slots from the days when it served the railroad trade as a hotel. The main dining room is cavernous, yet intimate. And the lounge proffers an atmosphere to satisfy the most civilized of those who engage in its liquid delights.

Whenever I first interview someone about their haunting, I approach what they offer me with caution, not wanting to be the victim of publicity seekers. As Nick and I sat talking together, he offered me a wee dram of a 17-year-old Bowmore Scotch. I can tell you this: any restaurateur who reserves this top Scotch for his guests is a man you may immediately trust. As we sipped away, the time we enjoyed together came to a close, and I asked Nick if anything odd had taken place in his restaurant recently.

> Well, something did happen just two days ago. I don't mind if the help uses the phone once in a while, but most of the calls from this area are long distance, and my phone bill was getting to be $50 or $60 a month more than it should be. So, I put a sign up next to the phone saying, "No Personal Calls." About an hour later I saw this busboy talking on the phone. It made me a little mad, and I went over and told him to hang up. After he did, I explained to him that there aren't supposed to be any personal calls being made. As soon as he walked away, the phone rang. When I picked up the receiver, this old man's voice said "for personal use only" in a real mocking tone. Now that's pretty strange, but even so, I still don't want to believe it was a

ghost—I'm always looking for rational explanations.

Nick was more than helpful in relating his strange tales. He even tuned me in to several others he said would have more substantive stories than his. As bad luck would have it, one former employee, now a restaurant manager with a national chain, was on vacation when I phoned, and another, who had decided that hairdressing was more appealing than waiting tables, had changed her phone to an unlisted number. As I had a deadline to meet, their experiences were necessarily left out of this account. I did, however, make contact with a pleasant woman named Jan, who is a reporter for the *Tri-County News*, a paper serving the general Flint area. Having spent a great deal of time in the Fenton Hotel, sometimes writing human interest stories about its haunting, and even attending a séance or two, she was able to substantiate just about every detail I have just related. In fact, she insists that at one séance the attendees managed to contact as many as seven spirits, all of them more than a little bit restless.

As this story comes to a close, the haunting continues. Cold drafts are felt in the coat check room, glasses continue to fly off the barroom shelves, and doors can be heard opening and closing. "Just last New Year's Eve," relates Nick, "one of our prep workers came in early, at about 3 A.M., to set things up for the day's festivities. As he was going about his duties, prepping the food, this man walked into the kitchen and right up to where he was standing, and then just disappeared. I darn near lost a prep man that morning."

One can easily understand why.

Postscript . . .

Just as this tale was being readied for the publisher, additional confirmation of the haunting of the Fenton Hotel floated my way. Denise Dillard, the former waitress I had a hard time tracking down because of a changed phone number, contacted me late one evening, excited to tell of her many encounters with the paranormal activity that came as a of fringe benefit at her former place of employment.

A petite, energetic woman with a most pleasant personality, Denise began by telling me about her first day at the old yet swank restaurant.

> I was waiting tables in the green dining room, already nervous about doing well on the job, when I felt someone squeeze my upper arm. When I turned around to see who it was, there was no one near me. Immediately, I went into the kitchen, quite shaken, and told the two cooks—one of whom was the owner, a man named John Lafferty—about what had happened. They acted like they really didn't believe me, but they were still sympathetic. Then, a few minutes later, it happened again, a firm grab of my upper arm. I totally lost it at that point and had to be sent home. I was in tears over that one.

A short while later, Denise was filling in as a hostess, working the posh foyer area. She encountered her second ghostly phenomenon.

> It wasn't a busy day, and it must have been around 4 P.M. I was sorting the menus and, all of a sudden, heard someone knocking on the wall inside the coat check room, which is directly in front of the front desk where I was standing. I went in to see who was doing it, and the knocking stopped. At that point I knew I was the only one in the immediate area, so I tried to ignore it, chalking it up to an overactive imagination. Then the knocking inside the coat room started up again, this time a bit louder. I real quick-like went to get a couple of my friends who were working with me that day so they could hear it, too. But when we got back to the coat room, the knocking had stopped again. We all stood there and listened for a while, but all was quiet. Then, as soon as they left, the knocking started up again. It really shook me up again, and I

Ghostly paintings of guests from earlier eras on the rear windows of the Fenton Hotel are a tribute to the site's haunted history.

ended up having to go home to compose myself.

After a while, Denise says she sort of got used to the ghostly shenanigans at the hotel, even when the spirits played games with her.

There's a blurb in the menu about the ghosts of the hotel. It tells about the man who orders a drink, and then disappears before you bring it to him. Well, that story is true, but it never happened quite that way to me. For me, I would be taking drink orders at one of the tables in the lounge, and as someone was telling me what they wanted, it was like I was hearing two voices giving me separate drink orders at the same time, and I couldn't tell what was what. So, I'd bring both drinks, and invariably I would have one drink left over—usually a whiskey sour or a whiskey and water. At first the bartenders didn't believe me, but I didn't care, it was really happening, so I'd tell them to put it on my tab and I'd take care of it. This happened to me several times in the lounge, never at the same table.

Denise confirms the haunting of her former place of employment and assures me that some of the events took place in front of customers.

One day, in mid-afternoon, I was talking to a customer named Rob about our ghost, Emery. Emery was an old man who worked at the place for many years and kept a room upstairs when the place was still a hotel. Throughout my years working there, I came to believe it was Emery who had singled me out for some reason as the target of his pranks. Anyway, I was telling Rob about Emery, and he was making it clear he wasn't buying into it. Then, it was like I could feel Emery standing nearby, and I said, "Emery's going to show you he's still here," and about a second or two later, the cash drawer at the bar where we were sitting opened up by itself. At the time, it was a new cash register, one of those electronic kinds where you have to push a button to get the drawer to open. We heard the beep of the button being pushed, and then the drawer opened up. That made a believer out of him.

One of the strangest and most fascinating tales about Emery concerns a group of two women and one man who came in one evening for drinks and snacks.

> It was a slow evening and these customers came in and sat in the lounge. There were three of them, and they had just gotten out of some sort of business seminar and were having drinks and something to eat. I remember hearing the man tell the women he didn't have any money on him, so one of the women loaned him $50. A few minutes later, I saw one of the women get up and go make a phone call. As the evening dwindled down, I went over and asked them if they'd like to have me cash them out. They sort of looked at me real strange like, and then they said someone had already cashed them out, that they had paid their bill. Since I still had their bill in my hand, I showed it to them, but they insisted they had already paid up, and the man showed me the change he had gotten back. The amount he had was exactly how much change he was supposed to get back, minus the 25 cents he gave one of the women for her phone call. I knew they weren't making this up, because they even offered to pay me again. The strange part was that they couldn't recall if it was a man or a woman whom they had paid—the best they could say was that they had paid "someone."

The Fenton Hotel was closed for a brief time about four years ago, so renovations could be undertaken. The day it shut down, Denise says she got an overwhelming urge to telephone the hotel.

> It was late on a Friday night, and I knew they were closed, and that no one was there, but I knew that if I'd call, Emery would answer. So I dialed the number, and sure enough, someone picked up the receiver. All I could hear on the other end was static, and so I said, "it's just me, Emery," and I heard the phone being hung up. I called right back again, but it just rang and rang. I know it was Emery who answered.

Denise worked at the hotel from 1977 to 1984 and

regularly visits the place to catch up with friends or to enjoy the great food. As recently as last February, Denise encountered Emery.

> I was in the lounge with friends and I could strongly sense Emery was with us. Sometimes when I'd go to the hotel I could tell he wasn't around, and sometimes I just knew he was. On this night, a Friday night, I knew he was present. There were only the three of us there that night, and I had told them I could sense Emery, that he was standing very near us. Then, we all heard a "ding" and when we looked over in the direction of the noise, one of the candles on the piano was suddenly completely engulfed in flames. When it died down, we went over to look, and the glass candle holder was split in two. It was only held together by the melted candle wax. Then, as we were getting our coats to leave, someone grabbed me by my hips and moved me to one side, like he was trying to get by me in a hurry. I instinctively stepped out of the way and looked behind me, but there was no one there. One of the people I was with saw me scooting to get out of the way, and asked me if Emery had just passed by. I told her that yes, it was him.

As if this story didn't have enough eerie happenings to satisfy the taste buds of the most ardent of ghost-hunters, it treats us to dessert as well. It seems there's a reason why disembodied Emery is enchanted with our darling Denise.

> I now work at the same hair salon as a girl named Stephanie, who happens to be Emery's granddaughter. One evening, she and I were at the lounge in the hotel, and Stephanie told me she had something to show me. She took out an old photograph of her grandfather and grandmother. I was shocked at how much Emery's wife and I looked alike. The resemblance was downright uncanny. What's more, I took a photo out of my wallet, a picture of my son. In the photo he's standing next to his father, my ex-husband. Now it was Stephanie's turn to be shocked—my ex-husband bears an absolutely striking resemblance to Emery. And as if that's

not enough, the photo of my ex and my son had been taken inside the Fenton Hotel.

Such supportive stories as these warm the heart of a tired old ghosthunter like myself, encouraging me to keep on keeping on. I plan to visit the hotel regularly.

13

Night Watchman

Place Visited: A two-story, wood-frame home, circa 1930, near the corner of north 13th Street and M-35 in the Upper Peninsula city of Gladstone

Period of Haunting: Indications suggest that this home has been haunted for the past 30 years and is most likely still experiencing paranormal activity.

Date of Investigation: Intermittent investigations between the years 1979-1984

Description of Location: The home is located in an area of Gladstone off-handedly referred to by locals as "The Buckeye," an area not within the city proper, but infamous for the many moonshiners who plied their trade in this neighborhood during Prohibition. From an upstairs bedroom window, I'm told one can enjoy a breathtaking view of Little Bay DeNoc, the northern-most point of Lake Michigan. The house itself has three bedrooms and a half bath upstairs, while the ground level presents a kitchen, L-shaped living room, bedroom, full bath, and utility room. There is no basement, as the house sits upon a crawl space. To reach the home in question, one must make the pilgrimage north through Michigan's Lower Peninsula and across the Mackinaw Bridge. As the "Yoopers," those residents of Michigan's Upper Peninsula, will firmly assert, you are now in "God's Country" and they will proudly proclaim that "God's area code is 906." Go west on US-2 through the pristine pines of the Hiawatha State Forest and in about two hours the highway will eventually divide, and you'll find yourself passing through the out-

skirts of Gladstone. At the intersection of US-2 and
M-35, turn right. Go under the railroad track overpass;
north 13th Street is the first street on your left. While
in the vicinity, be sure to visit the downtown area and,
in particular, The Dew Drop Inn (no kidding, that's its
name), famous with the locals for homemade cinnamon
rolls the size of Kentucky and so wonderfully sweet
you'll most likely need an insulin shot if you even come
close to finishing one. Be advised, it's probably best
to visit the area in the summer, as the cold and snowy
weather tends to come early and stay late. As the na-
tives say, "Up here, there are two weeks in August
when the ice fishing is pretty lousy."

The Haunt Meter: * * * * *

Gary and Tara Henley (not their real names) were
warned by friends not to purchase the two-story house
on north 13th Street. Local legend insisted it was
haunted and that no one ever seemed to live within its
walls for very long. In fact, at one time the place had
been boarded up for several years, and children passing
by on their way to school used to throw rocks at it in
defiance of the spirits who supposedly resided within.
Still, it seemed an ideal location for the two of them and
their three elementary-school-aged children, especially
since their children's school was just a short jaunt up
the bluff to the north. "Besides," says Gary, "I didn't
believe in any of that haunted house nonsense. In fact,
my response was 'As long as I'm making the payments
on the place, any ghost had better know how to get
along with me.'"

Rob, Rachel, and Neil, the Henley children, who were
aged 10, 8, and 6, respectively, during the height of the
haunting, were thrilled to have bedrooms of their own.
Gladstone was an ideal place for kids their ages, with
plenty of outdoor activities such as canoeing, fishing,

and camping. The fenced-in backyard provided a safe place to play with their friends or with their pet dog Duke, a shaggy, black and tan German Shepherd-Collie mix. For all intents and purposes, it seemed a great place to live, until, of course, a spectral visitor of the night began to manifest himself to the children.

"For several months," says Gary,

> we would put the kids into bed, and Tara and I would watch TV for a couple of hours. It seems that we were constantly hollering upstairs for the kids to get back into bed, as we could hear soft footsteps sneaking down the hallway above us. The kids would holler back that they weren't out of bed, but we just figured they were covering for one another.

It wasn't until almost a year after they had moved in that Gary and Tara became aware of something strange taking place in their new home. Sitting in the living room, they began to catch fleeting glimpses of a thin, dark shadow creeping its way up the stairs and toward their children's bedrooms. As eerie as it seemed, they passed such experiences off as shadows caused by the headlights of traffic passing by on the main road running immediately east of their house. "It was easier," Tara explains, "to believe in the reality of headlights through the curtains than ghosts climbing your staircase. And it wasn't long before we started remembering how our friends had warned us about how the place was haunted."

It was their daughter, Rachel, who first broke the silence about having a ghost in their home. "Had it come from Rob or Neil," says Tara, "we would've been reluctant to believe what we were hearing. But Rachel was always our studious one, the middle child who always did the right thing and stayed out of mischief. So when she finally came to us, we thought we'd best take what she had to say seriously."

Let's pause for a moment and let Rachel, now grown up and living with her husband and small son in Utica

Township, relate her story:

> Every night, Mom and Dad would put us to bed around nine o'clock on school nights or maybe ten o'clock during the summer. And every night "he" would come. Our bedrooms were all in a row, with mine in the middle and a long hallway running from bedroom to bedroom. Neil and I had beds situated in such a way that as you lay down, you faced the doorway looking into the hallway. Rob's bed didn't face his door, so he never saw what we saw, which was a good thing, because Rob always had a wild imagination and he would have totally freaked out over this.

> We'd lie in our beds, and not ten minutes after being tucked in, we'd see the shadow of a man moving across the wall of the hallway. First it would sort of shuffle over to Rob's doorway, where it would stand there for a few seconds, staring in at him as he lay in bed. Then it would move toward my room, where it would actually enter my room and stand next to my bed looking down at me. Usually, I was too afraid to look directly at it, but on those occasions when I did, I could see it was an old man, very thin and with deep, sunken eyes and a hawk nose. He would just stare down at me for a few moments, and then shuffle off down the hallway toward Neil's room. After staring at Neil for a minute or so, he would turn and begin to go back down the stairs, always fading away by the time he was halfway down. The impression I got was that he wasn't mean and that he wasn't trying to frighten us, but that he was simply checking on us to make sure we were all OK. But I was just a little kid then, and stuff like that scared the heck out of me. This went on nearly every night I lived there, at least until I moved my bed so I wouldn't have to see him anymore.

Having told her story to her parents, Gary and Tara took it upon themselves to approach their youngest son, Neil. "We didn't know exactly how to bring the subject up to a six-year-old," says Tara, "so we just asked him if he ever saw either one of us come upstairs to check on him after he had gone to bed. What he told us confirmed

Rachel's story and convinced us we truly did have a ghost in the house."

This time, let's allow Neil to recount the activities of their paranormal houseguests—a story given more credence by the fact that Neil is now a police officer with a down river Wayne County municipal police department:

> My story matches Rachel's exactly. Just about every night after Mom and Dad had tucked us in, I would see an old man walking up the stairs and into the upstairs hallway. First, he would take his time walking over to Rob's room. He was all bent over and it seemed hard for him to move very fast. He'd step just inside Rob's room, stand there a minute or two, and then turn and head toward Rachel's bedroom. Then he'd go all the way into her room where I couldn't see him. After a minute or so, he'd come back out and slowly start making his way toward my room. I never got a close look at him because about the time he'd get to my doorway I'd pull the covers over my head or I'd pretend to be asleep. I just wanted him to go away. I remember being terrified of opening my eyes and having him still be standing there in my doorway, staring at me. Usually, I'd go to sleep with my head under my covers. I was too afraid to even tell Mom and Dad about it.

Armed with the information about their nocturnal houseguest, Gary and Tara decided to check things out for themselves. "We decided to stake out the upstairs," says Gary. "Several nights we would tuck the kids into bed and then lie down next to them for a while—Tara in bed with Rachel and me in bed with Neil. We did this off and on for a couple weeks, but nothing ever happened. We figured that maybe the old man felt he didn't have to check on the kids if we were already in there with them."

Not certain what to make of their children's stories, all Gary and Tara could do was wait for clear evidence of their own that they had a genuine haunting on their hands. As it turns out, they didn't have long to wait.

"It was a beautiful spring day," recalls Tara.

Gary was at work and the kids were all outside playing
in the backyard with friends. Since it was all fenced in,
I didn't feel the need to stay out there with them all the
time, so I'd just check on them every few minutes or
so. During one of my checks I noticed Neil was
missing. The other kids were so engrossed in their play
that they hadn't seen where he had gone. I began to
call out his name, but I got no answer.

After a few minutes of calling out Neil's name, Tara
became frightened. A busy highway passed right by
their home, and just a block away was a wooded area
where a six-year-old could easily get lost. Frantic, Tara
knocked on her neighbor's doors, but everyone denied
having seen Neil. "I had my neighbor come over to watch
the kids in the yard," says Tara, "and I scoured the
neighborhood, but I still couldn't find him. I was shaking and in tears by the time I got back home, and I knew
I had to call Gary at work. I was certain Neil was gone."

Tara went into the kitchen and, trembling, picked up
the wall phone and began to dial her husband's place of
employment.

That's when I saw the old man. He just suddenly
appeared in the doorway between the kitchen and the
living room. I remember I wasn't frightened at all. In
fact, it all seemed strangely natural at the time. He
stood there looking at me for a moment, this gaunt,
stooped-over old man. He didn't say a word and in an
instant he was gone. Immediately I felt like he was
trying to tell me Neil was upstairs, so I literally flew up
the steps and there was Neil, lying on his bed, asleep.
It turns out he had gotten tired playing outside and
had just gone up to his room to take a nap without
telling anyone what he was doing, something he would
often do again in the future. When Gary came home
from work, I told him all about it, and we decided on
two things—first, we definitely had a ghost in the
house, and, second, it was a protective ghost, so we
didn't need to be afraid. But even though we were

comfortable enough with the old man, the kids never did get used to him and were afraid of him until the day we moved out.

An interesting side note to this haunting concerns my visit to this wonderful old home in Gladstone. Whenever I visit a home purported to be haunted, I usually make a thorough inspection of the entire place. On this occasion, Gary and I inspected each room, snapping photographs and jotting down notes as we went, until we ventured down into the crawlspace, where Gary said he had something interesting to show me. Flashlights in hand, we descended through a trap door in the laundry room and into the dampness of the darkness below, traversing the area on hands and knees, being careful not to bump our heads on the support beams above us.

What Gary had to show me that afternoon was indeed uncanny. It seems that a couple of months earlier he had been rolling insulation around the perimeter of the crawlspace, to ensure that his water pipes wouldn't freeze in the upcoming winter, when he discovered a large, wooden box partially buried beneath the dirt floor. Sure enough, I saw it too. It measured about 36 inches wide by about 20 inches high. How long it was we couldn't decide because only this one end was sticking up and out of the dirt. It looked for all intents and purposes like an old-time pine casket, with a thin plank lid, but, interested as I was, Gary was insistent about simply leaving well enough alone, and we made no attempt to pry it open. I did manage to snap two photographs of this unidentified artifact, but neither of them turned out well enough to see anything but blackness. I'd like to think it was just too dark down there for anything to show up on film, but I did have a flash on my camera, so I should have captured something for my trouble. Besides, all the other photos of the house came out just fine.

Gary and Tara remained in their home for another

couple of years, before a job transfer called for a change of address. They insist their former home was, and still is, haunted. I've made recent attempts through one of the grown children to contact the current residents of the home, but have thus far received no reply.

Postscript . . .

As this story was being compiled for shipment to the publisher, the current owners of the home in Gladstone phoned one of the former residents to confirm that the haunting continues. It seems they have a teenaged son who, like many Upper Peninsula youths, enjoys sports. Combine that hobby with a teenaged appetite, and the lady of the house was not surprised to often hear her son traipse down the stairs and into the kitchen for a late-night snack. While she didn't mind these nocturnal feedings, she did mind the pounding, charging steps awakening her at 2 A.M. So, one night as she heard those stairs being heavily trodden, she threw open the door to her bedroom, which is located near the bottom of the stairway, to let him know she was fed up with all the unnecessary noise. What greeted her was an empty staircase. Upon tiptoeing up to her boy's room, she discovered him fast asleep, and in the morning he denied ever having gone down for a snack after having gone to bed.

And there's more. It seems the man of the house has a friend who drops by every now and then, and they while away the midnight hours down in the kitchen, tipping a few beers, and jamming with their guitars. Around 3 A.M. on the night in question, they were interrupted by a deep, heavy sigh, which they said was like the sound a disgusted person would make. Both men heard it and looked behind them to see who was there. Seeing no one, they continued on, only to hear it once again, this time much louder. The shaken houseguest then asked, "What the hell was that?" and the response given him was, "Oh, don't mind that, it's only our ghost." At that point, the man decided it was time to leave, saying, "That's it, I'm outta here."

It's heartwarming or bone-chilling—depending upon your point of view—to know a haunting continues through transferred deeds and new ownership.

14

Don't Remodel What Isn't Yours

Place Visited: A nondescript, two-story farmhouse, probably dating back to the 1930s or earlier, on South River Road in Gladwin, Michigan

Period of Haunting: 1989-? Most likely this ghost is awaiting another period of renovation before making further appearances.

Date of Investigation: August, 1997

Description of Location: The occupants of this home prefer to remain at least reasonably anonymous. Therefore, the best I can say is that their home sits along South River Road, south of the city of Gladwin, not too far from Gladwin State Park. Gladwin, a community rich in Amish heritage, is a charming town, with many cute gift shops and some truly nice home furnishing stores. To reach this idyllic snapshot of average America, travel US-27 north past Clare, then head east on Highway 61 until the middle of town. South River Road will be on your right. If you motor up I-75 from Flint, get off on 61 east and go west to South River Road and turn left. By the way, many homes in this area fit our description, so let's be reluctant to knock on doors.

The Haunt Meter: * * * *

Fran and Allen Boucher (don't bother checking the phone book; I've changed their names) enjoyed living in this old farmhouse, as it had ample space for rambling and rambunctious kids. As their income began to increase, so did their desire to begin interior renovations. Herein lies our tale.

"The first thing we decided to do," says Fran, "was remodel a couple of the upstairs bedrooms. We wanted to put up drywall and strip off old linoleum and lay carpeting. Then, there was this small room up there we just used for storage since it had no closet. I got the idea it would make a nice sewing room, so I wanted to completely gut it and start all over again."

It was during the remodeling of the bedrooms that Fran and Allen began to notice strange goings-on. Usually, when employed in the physical task of ripping up old carpeting and screwing down 4' x 8' sheets of drywall, one works up quite a sweat, especially in late summer. That's why the Bouchers found it odd when the rooms would suddenly and inexplicably turn icy cold. "It was absolutely unreal," says Allen.

> There was no central air conditioning, and it was hotter than the blazes up there when we'd start—so hot we needed a fan just to move the air around. Then, after a half hour or so, the room would just turn freezing cold. In some places, like inside the closet of one bedroom, you could sometimes even see your breath, it was that cold in there.

With the bedrooms in shambles, even parapsychological phenomena was not reason enough to put a halt to the task at hand. Thus, every afternoon and evening for several weeks, the laborious chores continued. And so did the unnatural activity. Tools would disappear and hanging the drywall became more than just a nuisance. "We took forever to hang the drywall in those rooms," says Fran. "We'd go up there to work, and sometimes the drywall screws would be gone, and then the next day maybe it would be the drywall tape or the drywall mud. It seemed like something or somebody just didn't want the walls covered with drywall."

Allen was more aggravated by his disappearing tools:

What got really weird for me was when my tools began
to disappear on me. I'd get home from work, eat
supper, and then head upstairs for the evening. Things
would be fine at first, and then I'd reach for one of my
tools—one I had just been using—and it would be
gone. I began to lose screwdrivers, hammers, and even
my staple gun. And I had been the only one up there at
the time. This went on for several days, and I'd have to
get replacements out of my toolbox. Then, one day I
had to go into the basement for a can of paint, and
there, sitting on top of one of the ceiling support
beams, were my tools. They were lined up in a neat row
across the beam. After that, whenever a tool would
disappear, I'd go back downstairs and retrieve it off the
same beam. Now, tell me that's not damned strange.

Although these mysterious events continued on a
regular basis throughout the remodeling of the bedrooms, it wasn't until Fran and Allen began to gut the
spare room she wanted to use as a sewing refuge that
they actually encountered their ghost. Fran had decided
to clear out the room while her husband was at work
and began to haul boxes out into the hallway, stacking
them neatly against an upstairs wall. She had gone
back into the room for another armful, when something
caught her eye. Standing in the doorway, arms folded
and eyes peering right through her, was a slim man of
about forty years of age. He was wearing old coveralls
and a long-sleeved plaid work shirt. Although it was well
over 80 degrees up there, on his feet were winter boots.

I knew instantly that he wasn't real, that he wasn't
alive. He looked right at me, shook his head in disgust,
and turned and walked away. I've never been so
weirded-out in my life. I dropped what I was carrying
and ran downstairs and picked up the phone and
called my mother. I didn't tell her what happened
because I didn't want her to think I was nuts. But I
just needed to have a human voice speaking in my ear.

Not long after this, Allen and one of his daughters, whom I shall call Trisha, were present when the ghost once again went public. Trisha had accompanied her father to the basement to bring up clothes from the dryer. "It's not what I would really call a basement," says Allen.

> The floors are still dirt in some parts, and it has no possibilities for improvement. I have a workbench in one corner, and there's an old plank door that opens into what used to be used as a coal bin. It's old and damp and dirty down there. Well, Trisha and I had sorted the dry clothes into two piles, and each of us took an armful. When we turned away from the dryer, there he was, this tall man standing over by the doorway to the coal bin. He was staring at us, with a look on his face like he didn't approve of us being down there. I watched him for a moment, looked over at Trisha to see if she saw him too—which she did—and then looked back. He was still there, watching us. Without saying a word, we both headed for the stairs. As we made our way up, we could still see him standing there. Explain that to a 12-year-old girl.

Although obviously upset by the renovations taking place upstairs, the basement became the foreboding refuge of their critical spook. "I reached a point," says Fran,

> where I refused to go down there alone. No way. It got to where I would see this guy in a different spot just about every third or fourth time I went downstairs. So, after a while, no matter what I needed from down there, I waited until Allen came home and made him go with me. Even then, we spied him over by the coal bin door watching us a couple of times.

The Bouchers decided it was time to speak with the children about their new houseguest, basically to impress upon them the fact that it was in the best interests of the family to keep these experiences to themselves. After all, good people don't need questionable reputations. But something soon happened that exposed the spectre to the extended family.

Allen remembers:

> We were having a birthday party for one of our girls. Grandparents and aunts and uncles and cousins were over, and we had just dished out the ice cream. The kids all wanted cones, so we dipped them all out and sent them outside to play. As we adults were just sitting there drinking coffee and eating ice cream, we all heard these really heavy footsteps coming down the stairway from upstairs. We looked up, and this same tall, thin man came down the stairs and walked into the living room. Then, about halfway across the room, he stopped, turned toward where we were all sitting in the kitchen and sort of squinted his eyes at us. Then he turned back around and walked out of sight and into our bedroom. My cousin and I jumped up and went in there, but by then he was gone. That sort of blew our cover with the relatives. Some of them found it fascinating, others announced they'd start visiting again if we could prove this guy wouldn't be around any more.

It appears the skittish clansfolk didn't have to wait long to pay a repeat visit. Not long after Fran and Allen finished their remodeling project, the ghostly figure of the slim man in old work clothes stopped making his unexpected appearances. "I think he didn't like the fact we were tearing up his house," says Fran. "When we were all through, he went away."

Fran and Allen are content with how quiet their abode has become, and even trips to the basement are not as foreboding as they once were. However, there's talk now of remodeling the kitchen, and the Bouchers are more than just a little curious as to whether or not they'll once again be visited by their disapproving spirit.

15

Someone's in the Bedroom with Jason

Place Visited: A single-family residence on Ottawa Street in Grayling, Michigan

Period of Haunting: Ongoing

Date of Investigation: November, 1999

Description of Location: Grayling is hailed as a northern Michigan utopia for outdoor activities, and many "downstaters" keep summer homes in the area. It is surrounded by pristine forests and clear, cold lakes. Excellent fishing, hunting, and camping possibilities abound, and in the summer months the population of the area dramatically increases. Grayling gets its name from the prized game fish which used to frequent the pure streams and azure lakes of northern Michigan. If traveling the main route from Detroit to Mackinaw City on I-75, you'll pass right through Grayling. The house in question is located on Ottawa Street, which shouldn't be too difficult to find considering the moderate size of the city.

The Haunt Meter: * * * *

Everyone knows that when adolescents pass through the volatile stage of puberty, all sorts of odd behavior can surface. That's why the Cardwells, Sherrie and Pat, didn't pay too much attention to the stories their oldest son, Jason, had been spouting at the supper table in recent weeks. During that family time together, he had been filling them in on the visitor who was coming to his bedroom long after the household was supposed to be embraced in the restful arms of slumber.

"Jason always had an overactive imagination," says Sherrie, a friendly young mother of three. "Even before he started school, he would make up stories, draw pictures, and pretend to lead his friends on adventures as they played together in his room. So, when he began to tell us of seeing someone in his new bedroom at night, we didn't give it an awful lot of attention."

As a natural part of outgrowing his childhood, Jason had felt like spreading his wings a little bit and insisted he be given his own bedroom, that sleeping with his kid brother was now somehow beneath him. Honoring his request, Sherrie and Pat rearranged a spare back room and moved all of Jason's belongings into his new digs. Jason was delighted with his newfound sense of independence and enjoyed his moments of privacy away from the rest of the family, right up until he began to encounter the ghost who frequented his room after dark.

"The first time I saw him," says Jason, an unusually articulate youth with sparkling eyes,

> I was lying in bed with all the lights out. All of a sudden, I could see this man standing by my bedroom window, looking outside. There wasn't much light, but I could tell it was a man, and that he was probably about my dad's age. At first, I thought someone had come in my room—maybe my dad—but then I knew right away this was somebody I had never seen before. I said, "Who are you?" and this guy turned really slowly toward my bed and just started looking at me. Then he started to walk toward my bed and I got really scared and yelled at him. I told him he wasn't welcome here and, when I said that, he turned back toward the window and just disappeared. I couldn't sleep very much that night, but I was too scared to get out of bed, so I just stayed where I was.

Because his parents had dismissed his ghost story, after several nights of worrying about whether or not this strange figure would return, Jason decided to take matters into his own hands. One evening he rounded up the family pooch, Boswell, and led him toward the bedroom. However, it appears old Boswell balked when he got to the doorway of Jason's bedroom. Although Jason sat on the bed and bid his dog to enter the room, all Boswell did was prance and dance around outside the doorway, like he needed to muster up a little more courage before crossing the threshold. Dismayed at his best friend's refusal to join him, Jason retrieved some sausage snacks from the kitchen and re-entered his bedroom. He tried for several minutes to coax the dog in, waving treats before his face, but as badly as old Boswell wanted those snacks, there was no way he was going in that room. Still undaunted by his failed endeavors, Jason went to the utility room and brought back Boswell's leash. What ensued was a tug-of-war contest, with Jason pulling toward the door and Boswell tugging in the opposite direction. So intense was the struggle, that you can still see the scratches on the floor left by Boswell's paws.

Several uneventful nights slipped by, leading Sherrie and Pat to believe Jason's imagination had calmed down. Then it was Sherrie's turn to notice something strange within the confines of her son's bedroom. One afternoon, she was engaged in the routine task of doing the family's laundry. Heading down the hallway to retrieve the dirty clothes from Jason's bedroom, she noticed the family cat, Buttons, sitting just outside the doorway to the room, seemingly fascinated by something or someone on the other side.

> I stood for a moment and watched her. Every now and then she'd cock her head from one side to the other, like whatever she was watching was moving around in there. Then she flinched and raised a paw and started to hiss. I went ahead into the bedroom, and all seemed

calm to me, but the cat wouldn't come in when I called her, and she usually follows me everywhere. So I picked her up and tried to bring her into the room with me. When I did, she went wild trying to get out of my arms, and eventually broke free and ran down the hall and into the kitchen. That's when I began to suspect there really might be something strange going on in there, that maybe Jason wasn't making all this up.

A couple of nights after the cat incident, Jason was once again snuggled beneath the covers of his bed when the phantom suddenly reappeared at the window. This time, Jason decided to lie there quietly and just watch the man to see what he might do. After a few moments, though, the level of his fear began to rise, and he spoke to the ghost, telling him to leave. This time, however, the ghostly figure did not simply dissipate, but turned toward the bed and walked forward, reaching out his arms as though to embrace the youngster. Jason's scream vaporized the ghost and summoned his parents, who in turn switched on all the lights, searched through the house for signs of an intruder, and then sat by Jason's bed until he finally fell asleep.

Frightened at the thought of sleeping in his new bedroom, Jason took up sleeping quarters once again with his little brother. While he felt relatively safe back in his own room, it wasn't long before both Jason and his kid brother began to hear footsteps walking down the hallway as they lay in their beds awaiting slumber's call. Sherrie says:

> They came to me right away, and told me they were hearing things in the hallway. So I decided to spend the next few nights sitting in the dark at the end of the hallway, to see if there was any truth to what they were saying, or if being scared was playing games with their imaginations. About the third night of doing this, I realized they weren't making it up and it wasn't their imaginations. As I was huddled on the floor in the dark, I began to hear footsteps coming down the hallway, heading right my way. I didn't want to believe

what I was hearing, and immediately in my mind I started to make excuses for what it could be. But the steps kept coming straight at me, and when they got to the opening of the boys' bedroom, because of the nightlight in there, I could see the dim figure of a man. He stopped at their doorway, and I wondered why he wasn't continuing on until I realized that the reason he stopped was that he was looking at me. That's when I really got scared, but at the same time I got angry, because he was right outside the room where my children were sleeping. I stood up and pointed at him and hollered at him to get out of my house, and he disappeared. Then I went into the boys' room to check on them. They were still asleep, so I went to the kitchen and poured myself a glass of wine to steady my nerves.

The Cardwells have no idea why their house would suddenly be haunted. A friend in whom they confided suggested that perhaps all the energy passing through Jason as he struggled with puberty attracted the spirit; the friend asserted that most poltergeist experiences seemed to take place in homes with puberty-aged children. But this didn't seem to be a poltergeist experience, as there were no objects flying around the house or sudden outbursts of paranormal activity. This appeared to be a bona fide haunting, and the ghost seemed to be spiritually attached to that one particular bedroom.

Jason has now moved permanently back into his old bedroom. While the frequency of the haunting seems to have lessened, every now and then the boys complain about hearing the footsteps in the hallway, and Boswell still adamantly refuses to go in the back bedroom, neither for love nor dog biscuits. "There are still times I have to go in there," says Sherrie,

to clean up or to make the room ready for any overnight guests. Sometimes I sense a presence in there, and I feel like I can't get out fast enough. On the other hand, some of our relatives have stayed the night in there—we haven't mentioned the ghost, of course—

and no one's complained. Pat even volunteered to spend a few nights in there, and he's never encountered anything. Maybe the ghost is cooling down a bit on his rambling around, or maybe he just didn't like anyone staying permanently in what he thought to be his room. At any rate, we can live with little signs he's still around, but we're glad things have calmed a bit. I just hope Jason doesn't decide to try to sleep in that room again, because I'm afraid this guy won't like it. But on the other hand, Jason can't stay in his brother's room forever.

The Cardwells have no idea who their ghost is and only have theories as to why he suddenly appeared. The haunting continues.

Someone from the other side has been in this bedroom with Jason. Other photos in the house didn't turn out.

16

Some Ghosts Just Grow on You

Place Visited: A spacious, Victorian-style home on Dwight Street in Jackson, Michigan

Period of Haunting: Reports of this haunting began in the early 1970s, but may well predate this time frame. The haunting continues.

Date of Investigation: 1996-2000. It is firmly believed by the former residents of this home, that the haunting predated their tenure on Dwight Street and that, due to the nature of the haunting, the paranormal activity must certainly continue to this day. Past history has shown this to be an extremely haunted home, a veritable smorgasbord of phantasmagorical phenomena.

Description of Location: Since the family who related this information to this author no longer reside in the home, they have asked me not to include the exact address. They believe the current occupants most likely have their hands full with unwanted spectral guests and don't need the added aggravation of curious ghost-hunters gathering on their front lawn.   Jackson, in south central Michigan, is an All-American city located about an hour west of Detroit and about midway between Ann Arbor and Battle Creek on the I-94 corridor. It is a charming city in which to live, with such attractions as Ella Sharp Park, which offers acres and acres of manicured lawns, picnic plazas, tennis courts, and baseball diamonds. Not far from this idyllic greenery are the Cascades, a tumbling waterfall illuminated by a rainbow of lights, which has been entertaining citizens on warm summer evenings for decades. Jackson is also home to, in this author's opinion, the best hamburger palace in all of Michigan—Schlenker's, located on Ganson Street. Take my word for it, fast-food joints have to stand on their mother's shoulders to kiss Schlenker's behind, it's that good. But I digress. To reach the street in question, take I-94 either east or west, depending on your point of departure, to the US-127 South exit. Take US-127 south just a brief distance to the Michigan Avenue exit and turn right. Follow Michigan Avenue westbound until Dwight Street and turn left. Dwight Street is just east of Foote Hospital. The home is between Michigan Avenue and Plymouth Street.

The Haunt Meter: * * * * *

Wyatt and Carly Simmons (names changed, again) moved into their first new home in July, 1982. As Carly puts it, it was love at first sight. Although described by neighbors as being Victorian in style, the Simmons thought their new home more resembled a turn-of-the-century city fire station.

"From the street," recalls Carly, "the house was BIG. We had previously lived in a mobile home, so this place was cavernous. It was red brick with white-trimmed wooden windows, each of which was outlined by arched brick trim across the top. A spacious porch with white wooden pillars stretched across the front, an ideal place to hang a swing."

If Carly and Wyatt were pleased by the exterior, they became ecstatic upon entering the front door. "That door was solid oak," explains Carly,

> with a full beveled-glass window. Just off the front entryway was an open staircase of polished oak. At the foot of the staircase was an original leaded and stained-glass window. To the right of the staircase was

a huge living room with ten-foot ceilings and carved oak trim a foot wide. Two huge windows were also trimmed in heavy, carved oak. Standing near the front door, you could peek inside the dining room, which sported a partially-inlaid oak wall. The entry to the dining room was outlined in ornate oak pillars, and the dining room windows were also stained-glass with wooden shutters. Immediately off the dining room was a smaller room the realtor described as a music room, with old-fashioned, wall-sconce light fixtures.

When they first walked through the front door, Wyatt and Carly knew this was the house of their dreams. While they had looked at other houses, this one most like "home." A spacious kitchen filled the rear of the house and was completely remodeled with new cupboards and brown brick walls. Off the kitchen on the north side was a door leading to a small service porch, which in turned spilled out into the backyard. However, not all was idyllic within its walls. Carly says:

> There was a landing off the kitchen, with a door leading to the basement. This part of the house I never liked. It felt very eerie standing there on that landing. It was always cold and musty. Down in the first room of the basement there was a small workshop, and from there another door which opened up to the rest of the basement. The left side of the basement had a concrete floor, but the right side was slightly elevated, with a sand floor. In nine years of living there, I never felt that I belonged down there. I was thankful the laundry room was on the first floor, just off the kitchen. I may have given up laundry altogether had it been in the basement.

The second story included several bedrooms, a full bath, and a huge room that at one time had been a kitchen. It was a large house for just the two of them, but they knew it would be a great place to start a family. "The place was so beautiful," Carly reminisces, "that Wyatt and I often dreamed we would have daughters, and that they would some day descend that golden oak staircase in their wedding gowns."

As a newly-married couple, Wyatt and Carly didn't have nearly enough furniture to fill the enormous space. With very few furnishings, the house had an echo, and every little sound seemed amplified, resonating off the walls and pulsating from one room to the next. Still, they were excited about getting settled in.

"As with any new home owners," says Carly,

the first thing you tend to unpack is the kitchen stuff. You decide which cupboard gets used for plates and glasses and food items. We chose what we thought would be the most efficient set-up—but we didn't know we should have consulted with the ghosts of the house. Not long after we had moved in, I came down one morning to the kitchen to make coffee and all the cupboard doors had been tampered with. Some were wide open, while others were only slightly ajar. I was positive they were all closed when I had gone to bed, and upon closer examination I discovered everything inside the cupboards had been rearranged. I mean, the contents of each cupboard were now in completely different cupboards altogether. I asked my husband if he had moved anything, but he hadn't. So I moved things back to where they were and closed the doors. The next morning, everything was rearranged again. This went on for several weeks, this same puzzling sight greeting us every morning at breakfast. Eventually, I just gave up and gave in.

It seems the battle over how the cupboards ought to be arranged was only the beginning of their ghostly escapades. Soon, the two of them began to hear footsteps upstairs while they were in the den watching television. They joked about it, referring to the sounds as "the ghost upstairs," not realizing how accurate their assumption truly was. "In spite of all that had happened up to that point," says Carly, "we still didn't believe that our house was actually haunted. Don't ask me why. We just didn't."

Soon, Wyatt noticed some of his belongings had

begun to disappear. His pocket knife, some of his tools, and inexpensive jewelry items simply vanished. Carly noticed some of her trinkets missing as well, along with a gold wedding band her mother had given her. In spite of it all, they casually laid the blame on their cat, until things began to occur in which no feline could possibly have had a hand (or paw).

"We noticed," recalls Wyatt,

> that sometimes, when walking from the den to the dining room, we would feel a very noticeable drop in temperature. Even in the summer, there was a tremendous drop in temperature between the two rooms. Sometimes, it was only a small portion of the dining room that was cold. Not only was it cold, though, it was clammy. You'd actually get the chills passing from the den to the dining room.

About a year after settling into their new home, Carly gave birth to a daughter, Amie. Needing the extra cash, Carly returned to work a couple of months later and hired a young woman named Christine to watch the new baby. Carly and Christine soon became great friends, and Christine was considered a second mom to Amie. She would come over in the morning and watch Amie until either Wyatt or Carly returned home from work.

"One evening," remembers Carly,

> I came home from work and Christine stayed for supper. Wyatt was out of town, and the two of us chatted away into the late hours of the evening. Then, over coffee, Christine told me a story that made my eyes grow wide with wonder. She said that one day a few weeks earlier, she had put Amie down for her nap in the upstairs nursery. Then she had decided to lay down for a while in our bedroom, just off the nursery. Shortly after she had fallen asleep, she was startled awake by someone grabbing her leg and shaking it. This "someone" was saying, "Grandma, Grandma, wake up." At first, Christine thought maybe she was dreaming all this, but then, as she lay there wide awake, it happened again. It spooked her so bad she

jumped out of bed and raced into Amie's room, to find her peacefully dozing away. She said it took her several hours to get herself back together, and that she decided never again to nap in our bedroom.

Immediately, Carly began to connect Christine's encounter to the footsteps, the missing trinkets, and the kitchen cabinet fiasco.

It was at this point, that I knew we had a ghost in the house. In fact, just a day or two later, something began to occur which convinced even Wyatt. We would put Amie in her baby swing—the kind you would crank up—and let her swing away until she would fall asleep. Well, when the swing would wind down, we'd hear Amie begin to whimper, so we'd get up to go crank the swing back up. Each time we'd get up to do so, we'd hear the crank turning, and by the time we'd get there, Amie would once again be swinging away, and sleeping peacefully.

Carly and Wyatt soon realized that at least one of their ghosts was very much attached to their daughter. Carly recalls:

One night when Amie was about four years old, she didn't want to go to bed, so I asked her if she was afraid to go upstairs. She answered "no," and told me that Grandma was always up there with her and would sing to her and rock her until she had fallen asleep. I knew there had to be truth in this, because there were many times when I'd check on Amie and would find the rocking chair in her room gently coming to a halt, as if someone had just gotten up from it.

Still feeling very much at peace with their ghosts, Carly and Wyatt went on with life as usual. Enjoying company and loving to host theme dinner parties, Carly often found herself immersed in food preparation in her kitchen.

This is when the new hobby of our "extended family" began to exhibit itself. As I would be cooking in the kitchen, certain appliances would just stop running.

Not the entire kitchen as a whole, just a mixer or the microwave or the blender. All the outlets were on the same circuit, and the wiring in the house had just been updated. Besides, I would have these appliances operating at the same time, and they would take turns shutting off. Then, as I'd pause to deal with this inconvenience, my party platters would disappear, sometimes even the ones with food on them. This sort of thing only happened when I had a lot of guests coming over. Then I'd leave the room to check on Amie, and when I would return, my missing platters would be back on the kitchen table. It was aggravating, and more than a bit eerie, but the sense I got of it was that our ghosts wanted to be included, that they were being playful.

Wyatt and Carly insist they never felt threatened by their ghosts, whom they decided must be grandmother and granddaughter, and finally settled into the idea that, since neither they nor their ghosts were going to leave, they might as well learn to get along with one another. During the time spent together, grandmother and granddaughter would consistently toss in little clues as to their existence, stepping up the paranormal activity. Carly insists there was hardly a day when something strange didn't take place, but that the spirits were actually somewhat comforting to have around. Theirs was an old house, so they believed they had an old haunting going on, and they began to wonder about the history of the house, and why their ghosts were so insistent on sticking around.

One summer's day, a few years after having moved into the house, Carly held a rummage sale. An elderly man strolled up the lawn, saying he was drawn to the sale by an antique library table Carly was using for display purposes. The table wasn't for sale, but Carly and the old gentleman struck up a conversation. Let's allow Carly to relate what happened next.

He asked us how long we had lived in the house and where we were from. After some time, he asked if he could go inside and look around, that as a child he and his parents had been invited to the house for a party. So, we took him inside, and he indicated that this was indeed the house he had visited as a youth.

He spoke of how the owners of the house had removed all the furniture from the living room to make space for the dancing. The dining room and kitchen were full of fine foods and wonderful drinks. He said the music room was where all the kids gathered to play while the adults visited and danced. Then he told us the strangest thing. He said he knew for a fact that the home had burned down when he was a young man. Yet here he stood, telling us that our house looked exactly the same as it did when he was a child, long before it had caught fire and been destroyed. Even the wood trim, the curved staircase, and the stained-glass windows were exactly as he had seen them as a child.

At this point, I asked him if he knew anything about the people who lived in the house at that time. All he could remember was that they were a well-to-do couple and that they were well known for the parties they would give. He said he believed the woman of the house had died in the fire. Now we were as intrigued as ever about our haunting.

Wyatt and Carly's attempts to check out the history of the home were in vain. Nothing about its history seemed to make any sense. Their abstract said the house was built in 1942, but the basement foundation was decades older, and the style of the house and original woodworking clearly dated back to the late nineteenth century. In fact, only the bathrooms seemed as modern as 1942 decor. (This makes the author wonder, can houses be reincarnated? Nah.)

Though the Simmonses made every effort to keep their haunting under wraps, it wasn't long before the relatives caught on. Carly had given birth to another daughter, Alexia, and her niece and niece's husband were to be godparents. During one visit, niece Kelly and husband Tony slept on a mattress on the floor of Amie's room. Late into the night, they were both awakened by the sound of a woman singing. Staring into the moonlit darkness of the room, they could plainly see the solid shadow of an elderly woman sitting on the edge of Amie's bed. Tony, frightened more than any man cares to admit, exited the room and took up residence on the living room couch for the remainder of the night. Kelly waited until the woman vanished, then awakened Amie and asked her about this strange serenader. Amie, about six years old at the time, matter-of-factly announced that there was nothing to be afraid of, that it was just Grandma, and that Grandma liked to sit on the bed at night and sing her to sleep.

While Carly insists they never felt frightened by their ghosts, her sister, Josephine, tells another story:

One night I had come over to Carly's house to help her hang wallpaper in Amie's bedroom. It was late when we finished, and I decided to stay the night, so they put me up in the guest bedroom on the second floor. Around 2 A.M. I was awakened by a choking sensation. I jumped out of bed in a panic and found myself engulfed by smoke. I ran out the bedroom door and down the hall toward Carly's room to wake them up because I was sure there was a fire. When I got out into the hall, I noticed there was no smoke out there, that it was only in my bedroom. I sneaked into everyone's bedrooms and they were just sleeping away like babies. The house itself was deathly still and quiet, and when I crept back to my bedroom, it was still filled with smoke. As I stood there, absolutely dumbfounded by what was going on, I realized the room was freezing cold. If there were a fire, it should have been blazing hot in there, but it was icy cold. And besides that, while I was engulfed in smoke, there wasn't a trace of the smell of smoke anywhere. Again, I couldn't breathe in there, so I stepped back out into the hall. I remember feeling dazed and confused, and then when I looked back into the bedroom, it was perfectly clear, not a whisper of smoke anywhere.

The next morning, when Josephine told of her smoky encounter with the mysterious unknown, both Carly and Wyatt maintained their silence about their haunted home. "My sister is very devoutly Catholic, so I didn't know if I should tell her about all the things we had happen to us," says Carly. "We didn't want her to think we were sacrilegious, or that we were having flashbacks to our '60s and '70s youth."

During the next two-and-one-half years, Carly and Wyatt would encounter the smoke themselves from time to time. Sometimes it would appear in the same upstairs bedroom and sometimes on the staircase between the first and second floors. In the meantime, the haunting continued; trinkets disappeared and footsteps were heard treading the upstairs hallway. "It just kept picking up in intensity," says Carly.

> We acquired an old player piano at a garage sale and placed it in the living room. Every once in a while, we'd lie in bed and listen to some unseen fingers plinking away on the keys. When we'd go down to investigate, we'd walk through cold, clammy spots in some of the rooms down there. Amie heard it, too, and told us that Grandma liked to play the piano at night.

Amie had been speaking of "Grandma" in affectionate terms since she had been old enough to talk. It was obvious she saw this elderly spirit frequently and would often speak to her while alone in her room. Soon, it was Carly who was about to encounter Grandma on her own.

> One night, I was sitting in a rocker in the living room nursing Alexia. Wyatt was at work, and Amie was upstairs asleep in her room. I heard someone coming down the staircase and just assumed Amie had woken up. I got out of the rocker to have a look and was astounded by what I saw. On the staircase was the upper portion of a woman dressed in light-colored clothing. Her neckline was high, and her outfit was extremely feminine, with lots of lace. She was coming

down the last few steps. Her hair was long and gray, and she looked very old. The vision was not solid, it was more like a vapor. I don't remember actually looking through her, but I think I may have been able to. She never came into the room, she just stayed on the stairs. I stood there with my baby in my arms and just stared at her. I wanted to speak to her, but when I finally got hold of myself to speak, she vanished. Just like that, she was gone. What was she doing? Why was she there? Did she come down to check on Alexia and me? Did she disappear because she saw we were all right? A thousand questions filled my head, and I still don't have an answer to any of them.

In the months that followed, Wyatt and Carly began to hear whispering voices drifting down from somewhere upstairs. They described it as two female voices, one elderly and one youthful, talking together. Now, more than ever, they were intrigued by their haunting. Were the two women truly granddaughter and grandmother? Was the smoke they encountered in the house residue from a disastrous fire decades earlier? Slowly, they began to believe the strange events were connected to one another.

Sadly, the Simmonses reached a point in their lives when they knew they had to move out of the home they loved. It wasn't the haunting that pried them away, but the offer of a better job for Wyatt. With heavy hearts, they began the process of packing up their belongings and preparing themselves for moving day.

"Just before we moved up north," says Carly,

my sister Josephine was over and was helping me pack boxes. My neighbor, Mike, came over to see if we needed help, and we got on the subject of our haunted house. He said he always wanted to ask us if we were aware the place was haunted. He said that the couple who lived in the house before us had told him all sorts of stories about the place, but he never wanted to tell us because he didn't know what our reaction would be. He said that one time they had come over to his place, scared out of their wits because their dining room had filled with smoke. It was just in the dining room, they said, and the smoke never drifted past the doorway. He said this couple couldn't take any more of the haunting and moved out. That's when we bought the place.

Neighbor Mike asked Carly and Wyatt if they knew any of the history of the house. Playing dumb, they let Mike fill them in. It seems that long ago, back in the '20s or '30s, the old lady who lived there was watching her granddaughter for a few days. The place had caught fire, and the little girl could be heard screaming at her grandmother to wake up. Both the old woman and the young child perished. Carly believes that explains the smoke in the various rooms of the house, as well as the little girl who pulled at her babysitter Christine's leg in the hope of awakening her grandmother.

Alas, moving day arrived. The trucks were loaded with personal belongings, leaving the house on Dwight Street as empty as the day they moved in. "Wyatt went back into the house to do a walk-through," says Carly, "and when he went down into the basement, there, on a shelf we had to duck underneath each time we walked from one basement room to another, were all the trinkets we had lost over the years. They were lined up in a neat row, not a speck of dust on them. We're convinced our ghosts, who by now were a part of our extended family, were saying good-bye. It felt like they were making a peace offering or were letting us know how much they loved us and would miss us."

Packed and ready to leave, the kids secure in the car with their aunt and uncle, Wyatt and Carly couldn't resist one last stroll through their dream home. Hand in hand, they visited each room, saying good-bye, their minds wafting back through a myriad of pleasant memories. They recalled the first day they had seen the house, the day they moved in, the laughter and the tears shared within its walls, the birth of their two precious daughters, the parties and the get-togethers with family and friends, and the special moments when they had encountered their "hostesses." It was a melancholy moment.

"As we walked hand in hand out the front door," remembers Carly,

> Wyatt propped the screen door open and called inside to Grandma and granddaughter. He told them we were all ready to go, and he asked them if they'd like to come with us to our new home. Then we waited on the front porch for several minutes, just sitting in silence on the porch swing, tears streaming down our faces. Then, Wyatt got up and closed the door, and we both drove off with heavy hearts. We knew they had decided to stay with their beloved house, and somehow I think they also had tears rolling down their spectral faces as they watched us drive out of sight.

This brings an end to the haunting experiences of the Simmons family. They are convinced, however, that it does not bring an end to the haunting of the house on Dwight Street in the city of Jackson—a home they loved, blessed by spirits they treasured.

17

The Lady in
the Window

Place Visited: A sprawling, beautifully-maintained, Victorian-style home in Jonesville, Michigan

Period of Haunting: 1986-present

Date of Investigation: Late October, 1987

Description of Location: Historic Jonesville was one of the stops made by stagecoach passengers as they rattled their way between Detroit and Chicago on what was then the main route between those port cities. That stretch, now called US-12, is still heavily traveled. A charming city, Jonesville is nestled within the rolling farmland on the outskirts of what are called The Irish Hills. It boasts a picturesque city park near its downtown shopping area, and this general area of Michigan draws great throngs of people to its many antique shops. Coming up from Indiana on I-69, exit at Coldwater, then head east a few short miles. It is about an hour and twenty minutes straight west from Detroit and about five minutes north of Hillsdale.

The Haunt Meter: * * *

Although this story is brief, it is nonetheless intriguing, especially as it comes from a police officer of impeccable reputation who is not desirous of media attention.

It was a crisp October afternoon, and the soft scent

of imminent rain was gently wafting from the west, when police officer Dave Richardson heard a call go out over his squad car radio, instructing a fellow officer to respond to a trespassing complaint within the city limits. Since he was already in the neighborhood, Dave radioed in that he would handle the call himself.

Dispatched to an immaculate, Victorian home with well-manicured lawns in the area of Franklin and Fayette Streets, Dave reached the address a couple of minutes after having received the call. "Kids were all over the place," says Dave, "as school had just let out and they were on their way home. It was near Halloween, and you could just sense the excitement in their voices as they skipped down the sidewalks."

Dave pulled his cruiser into the driveway of the home and exited with notebook in hand. The leaves had turned bright shades of gold and red, blanketing the front yard in autumnal hues.

As I stepped out of the squad car and toward the covered front porch of the house, I saw the curtains in one of the upstairs windows separate, and an elderly woman peered out at me. She had snow-white hair and was wearing a blue dress with white lace at the neck and wrists. She looked like she could be anyone's idea of what a kindly old grandmother should look like. At the time, I didn't suspect anything at all unusual about her.

Dave knocked on the door, and was greeted by a slim, attractive woman about 35 years old. Standing next to her was her elementary-school-aged daughter. Ushered into the living room of this spacious house, he was offered a seat, and after an exchange of pleasantries, began taking his report.

As it turned out, this lady wasn't really upset all that much. It seems the kids in the neighborhood would cut across her lawn a bit too often on the way home from school, and lately a couple of them had been using foul language as they did so. She just wanted me to make a report about it in case she had to call the mothers herself. She wanted something to back up her claims that some of the kids were getting a bit too rowdy. It was all pretty much just typical, small-town stuff.

Dave wrote down the woman's report, and then asked if the daughter knew what had taken place that day. Since she hadn't, he decided to ask if the woman upstairs had witnessed this minor indiscretion.

I asked if I could speak with the lady's grandmother. She just looked at me and asked me why on earth I would need to talk with her. When I replied that maybe she had seen something, I was told that it would have been impossible, as her only living grandmother resided in Jackson, 45 minutes away. That's when I mentioned to her that I had seen an elderly woman upstairs and just assumed it must have been her grandmother. That's when this woman got a really weird look on her face—sort of a cross between fear and astonishment.

"You've seen her, too?" she asked, in a voice filled with amazement. Dave replied that certainly he had seen her, as she had stood in front of the upstairs window and watched him walk up to the house.

That's when this lady really got nervous and she asked me if I could go upstairs with her and check out the room where I saw her. I figured something strange must be going on, so I followed both her and her daughter up the winding staircase and then down a beautifully-paneled hallway to the front, corner bed-room. When she opened the door to the room where I had seen her, there was no one to be found. But she did show me an antique photograph of the woman who had owned the place long, long ago. She said she kept the photo in the room because it fit the decor so well, as all the furnishings seemed to be from around the early part of the century. The woman in the photo was the woman in the window.

Before he left the house, report in hand, Dave discovered he wasn't the only one who had seen this elderly woman staring out the upstairs window. Neighbors had reported passing by on pleasant evenings and being watched by a woman who would part the curtains and stare at them as they went on their way. Additionally, the current owner told of how she and her family would return from an evening out, and, as they pulled in the driveway, would sometimes catch a glimpse of this same woman, as though she were waiting for them to return home.

According to Dave, the house in question is probably still haunted. The same family resides in the home, but they seek no public attention and would rather no one knew their exact location. "They're really good, down-to-earth people," says Dave, "and if they say they still see the same old woman I saw standing in that bedroom window, then I have no business doubting them."

18

Why Can't a Church Be Haunted?

Place Visited: A rural, country church, dating back well into the past century, spiritual home to about 100 folks who love to worship, and at least one ghost that still wishes to join them.

Period of Haunting: Rumors of this haunting go back several decades. According to the pastor, a great deal of activity is recent and ongoing.

Date of Investigation: July, 1999-August, 1999

Description of Location: Out of respect for the dedicated congregation, I will not divulge the exact location of this parish church. What I can say is this: 1) It is located within a 25-mile-drive of Lansing; 2) it serves the folks of a lovely, small community; 3) a photo of the haunted staircase is provided. Sorry, this is the best I can do, especially since I am intimately acquainted with the pastor of this church and wish him no undue strain within his parish. Besides, wouldn't it be fun to find this place on your own? Please note: names have been changed to protect the faithfully frightened.

The Haunt Meter: * * * * ½

When Tom Baird arrived at this church a couple of years back, he was fully prepared to minister to the needs of its congregation. He immediately fell in love with both the people and the worship facility and believed himself prepared, both professionally and spiritually, for whatever came his way. That is, until he began to hear about the haunting.

> I hadn't been here more than a month, when this lovely woman in her 50s asked me right out of the blue if I'd seen the ghost yet. I was a little taken aback, so I just smiled and asked her to tell me more. She said that she had attended this church basically all her life, and that for many decades now it has been haunted by the presence of a man. She spoke of how folks would constantly hear banging sounds and footsteps, and that once in a while some fortunate soul would actually catch a fleeting glimpse of the ghost they affectionately refer to as Billy.

Rev. Baird listened to the woman's stories with a disguised sense of humor, intrigued not so much by what he was hearing, as by the person he was hearing it from. "This was, and is, a pillar of the church community," says Baird, "a lovely lady with a gentle spirit. The sort of person every pastor wishes he had more of in his congregation. So, after listening to what she had to say, I decided to just keep an open mind."

An open mind was just the ticket for Rev. Tom, because in the next few weeks he encountered no less than five other persons who approached him independently of one another to ask if he had met the resident ghost. By then he was prepared to take the haunting seriously. "I could tell some of these folks were a little nervous about bringing this up," says Tom. "And a couple of them appeared to be a little frightened by it all. So I began to figure there must be something to all this after all."

Tom keeps an office in the back corner of the building, separated from the sanctuary by a fellowship hall area.

> If the sanctuary doors are open and if my office door is open, then I can see practically all the way across the full length of the church. I can't tell you how many

times I've been alone in the building and have heard someone moving around out in the church. All the sounds are different. Sometimes it sounds like someone just came in the side entry door, because I can hear it bang shut and then hear footsteps. Sometimes it sounds like someone is in the fellowship area moving some of the furniture around, although when I look out there everything is in its proper place. At first, I just passed it all off as the power of suggestion, but as I became more acquainted with the building I knew something was clearly amiss.

Ed Collingwood is the president of the men's society at the church. This group meets once a month early on a Saturday morning for breakfast, prayer, and a time of fellowship and service to the community. Ed, retired for several years from his position with a local municipality, finds the haunting strangely amusing:

I can't tell you how many times I've encountered our ghost. I'm usually the first guy here on Saturday morning, as it's my job to open up the church, go upstairs to the kitchen, and start getting breakfast ready for all the other guys. The volunteers who help me usually show up about a half an hour after I get there. Well, time and again I'll hear the door open and close downstairs, but no one comes up to help me. When I go to check it out, I'm the only one in the building. Sometimes, I actually hear someone coming up the stairs, which lead right up to the kitchen doorway, but when the walking stops, no one is there.

A former youth director at the church, a woman now in her mid-50s, insists the haunting is genuine. Let's call her Mary, for the sake of privacy.

One time, about ten years ago, a group of kids was spending the night in the church as part of a fundraiser. I was one of the chaperones, so I saw to it that the kids all stayed in the same section of the church together, so they wouldn't wander off. We had all sorts of activities for them in the fellowship area on the main floor, and the food was prepared in the kitchen upstairs. Those were the only areas of the church the kids were allowed to be in. We took all the kids upstairs for their treats, and I went downstairs to use the restroom facilities. When I crossed the fellowship area, I could hear a voice coming from the sanctuary, which was off limits. I went in there to round up whoever was in there, and the lights were all out. The voice was coming from near the choir loft, so I switched on the lights. When I did, the talking stopped, and there were no kids in the sanctuary at all—they were all upstairs and accounted for. Later that night, another chaperone heard the same thing when she went down to use the restroom. We decided not to tell the kids about it, but we also decided we weren't going to be a part of any more overnight events at the church.

The secretary of the church is an unassuming young woman named Missy. Her position is part-time, keeping her busy in her office three days a week, usually in the morning hours.

My office was originally the church library and pastor's office. It's a huge area, lined with bookshelves stuffed with Bibles and books that are very old—some of them over 150 years old. Directly above me is the kitchen of the church, and more times than I'd like to admit I hear someone walking around up there. I just do my best to ignore it, or tell myself it's just an old building with lots of creaky floorboards, but I know I'm not alone in there sometimes. In fact, I refuse to go into the church alone after dark. I know there's a ghost in there, and I don't want to see him, and I hope I never do see him. It's enough just to hear doors open, or to hear footsteps going up the stairs just outside my office.

The haunting of this place of worship goes way back, as the old-timers of the congregation spin stories of how their parents encountered the spirit long ago. In fact, many of the witnesses to this haunting are now deceased themselves. The legend that has been passed down through the last couple of generations holds that back near the turn of the century there was some church renovation going on. During this construction phase, one of the men of the church was busily hammering away near the top of the new bell tower when he slipped and fell, erasing himself from the membership roll. Yet, he supposedly remains in attendance just the same. As near as people can tell, the man's name was "Billy." Everyone acquainted with the haunting just assumes he is the culprit responsible for all the paranormal tramping about, but no one knows for sure.

"We had some furnace problems last winter," relates Rev. Tom.

> The repairman showed up, and I led him down to the basement where the furnaces are. Even if the building weren't haunted, that basement is creepy enough to make you think otherwise. Well, he started his work and I went back to my office. A few minutes later, he knocked on my door and seemed a bit upset by something. It seems he would set down one of his tools, and when he would reach for it again, it would be gone. Then the lights in the furnace room would shut off on him, and he'd have to go switch them back on again. About the third time the lights went out, he'd had enough and headed up the basement stairway to go get me. As he came up the stairs, he found his missing hand tools lying on one of the steps. The poor guy was scared silly, and I had to go back down there with him until he finished his work.

Rev. Baird believes that on more than one occasion, while he was alone in the church, the ghost was very near:

> One morning I got to my office early, about 7:30. I was doing some word processing on my computer, and my office door was open so the heat from the fellowship area would drift in. I hadn't been there fifteen minutes when I started hearing the entry door over by the secretary's office open and close and footsteps going upstairs. I thought it was awfully early for someone to

come in, but that maybe somebody needed to drop something off in the kitchen on their way to work. I went upstairs, because that's where I had heard the footsteps and the moving about, but there was no one there. I headed back down to my office, but when I reached the fellowship area, I could plain as day hear the furniture being moved around. It was so strange—nothing at all in the room was moving; it just sounded like it was. Then, I could hear the sound of papers rustling, like someone was going through a stack of paperwork. That sound was coming from a table about five feet away from me. It was like there were two of us at work that morning, but I was the only one in the building. I guess the noises went on for about ten minutes and then suddenly stopped. And this sort of thing has happened more than once, usually in the morning, but sometimes I've encountered this sort of thing at night.

The ghost of this church appears to wander the premises at will. Apparently, several of the parish members have actually spied the spirit, but they are reluctant to talk about it. After all, not everyone is comfortable with meeting a ghost, and a few folks are downright afraid that if they talk about it, it will happen again. However, one recent encounter had such a powerful effect on those who witnessed it that they felt a definite need to share the experience.

Loretta and Jackie are two good friends who are actively involved in the women's society of the church. During the 1999 Christmas season, they had gathered donations of clothing and personal hygiene items for a local shelter where women in the community flee from domestic abuse. They agreed to meet at the church, just a few days before Christmas, to pack the items into boxes and wrap them as gifts.

Loretta arrived at the church well after dark, just as Jackie was pulling into the parking lot with her three young sons. They exited their cars, everybody headed toward the church, arms laden with boxes of donated goods. As they entered the foyer, Loretta flipped on the light switch. A flash of yellow light streaked across the foyer, and the popping sound accompanying it indicated they had blown the circuit breaker. Standing in utter darkness, Jackie announced that she would go down the basement steps to the breaker box, and that her three boys, familiar with the turf, were to head on upstairs and deposit their boxes in the kitchen. "The kids had been up there a million times," says Jackie. "Their Sunday School classes are held up there, and their Cub Scouts meet there, too. So, I wasn't worried at all as they headed up the stairs, even though the lights were out."

The boys, boxes in tow, scampered up the stairs, in accordance with their mother's bidding. They made it about halfway up when they began screaming. "I had just gotten to the breaker box," says Jackie,

> when I heard the kids start screaming and running down the stairs. I reset the breaker switch and ran back to the foyer. My two youngest were literally clinging to Loretta's legs, scared to death. My oldest was still coming down the steps, only he wasn't afraid at all, he was fascinated. He told me that they were going up the stairs like they were told, when they saw a man standing at the top of the steps, just watching them. He said the man was sort of floating above the floor, and that he then turned and scooted into the kitchen area. His brothers had started screaming and running, but he remained there by himself for a moment until the man disappeared. He actually thought it was cool.

The two women were convinced the boys had seen a ghost. "Both Loretta and Jackie assured me," says Rev. Baird,

> that they had never said anything in the past about ghosts in front of the boys. They were so concerned about what had happened that they immediately tried to make it a positive experience, telling the boys that

he must be a good ghost if he lived in a church and that they were really lucky to be able to see him the way they did. What's funny is that when Jackie asked her kids what he looked like, they all agreed that he was a big man and that he was old. When asked how old they thought the ghost was, they said he was at least as old as I am. Well, I'm only 46 years old.

It appears that the haunting of the church continues on, without much break in the action. In fact, a recent youth activity involved the kids camping out on the church lawn for a night. When the weather suddenly became unseasonably cold, the usual spring rain turning to snow and sleet, the youth directors opted to remain outdoors rather than take the group inside for the night. Although the kids were mostly unaware of the haunting, the adults were all well aware of it and didn't want anything to do with a possible paranormal encounter.

"I'm kind of at ease with the haunting," says Rev. Tom. "There are times I wish he would actually show himself to me and there are times—especially when I'm alone in the building after dark—when I hope he doesn't show up. But I suppose that if I'm on the list to see him, I won't have any choice in the matter. After all, he's been here for years, and I guess he has just as much right to wander around this old building as I have."

At the top of this staircase in a long-haunted church, three young boys encountered a floating male ghost.

19

The Old Man in the Corner

Place Visited: A single-family dwelling on north Harrison Street in Ludington, Michigan

Period of Haunting: 1995-present

Date of Investigation: December, 1998

Description of Location: Snug up against the shores of Lake Michigan, Ludington is a vacationer's dream. Beautiful parks and beaches are proof one need not drive farther north to breathe in the picturesque beauty of tall pines and blue waters. In the winter, Ludington is perfect for snowmobilers, and deer hunters are drawn to the area for some of the finest hunting the peninsula has to offer. Motorists should take their time to reach Ludington. To rush would be to ignore the captivating scenery along the Lake Michigan coastline. Simply steer your vehicle westbound on I-96, through Grand Rapids and beyond, until the freeway spills you northward onto M-31. Continue up the coast until M-10 and head west. M-10 will turn into Ludington Street as you enter town. Remain on Ludington until Harrison and turn right. Somewhere on this stretch of residential bliss sits a genuinely haunted house.

The Haunt Meter: * * * * ½

Bob and Kay Erwin (not their real names) thoroughly enjoy life in Ludington. They've worked hard to make a good life for their children and have provided for them rather well. The wonderful old house in which they abide is more than a structure of wood and shingles; it is where they have crafted their memories and cast forth their dreams.

The Erwins have always opened their home to friends and relatives, and it was never unusual for their children to bring home classmates for supper or overnight visits. As receptive as they've always been, they were nonetheless apprehensive about a new visitor who showed up one spring afternoon—an elderly man who would suddenly materialize in the living room, only to inexplicably vanish before their wondering eyes.

"The first time it happened," says Bob,

> I was sitting on the couch watching the Tigers play on television. Kay had gone to the grocery store, and the kids were somewhere outside playing with their friends. Just all of a sudden like, I got the strong feeling I was being watched—you know what I mean, that nervous, uncomfortable feeling you're not alone. Well, I glanced back behind me, and there was this old guy, standing up tight against the corner of the room, just looking at me. I thought to myself, "who the heck is this guy and what's he doing in here?" Then I turned my eyes away for just a quick second, and when I looked back he was gone. It was unbelievable. It was just some old guy, and he never said a word. He just stared at me like he was lost or something. It was so strange. I could hear the birds chirping outside, and the kids playing down the street, you know—everything was normal, but here was this guy.

Bob shared his experience with Kay, but she hadn't had anything strange like that happen to her. It wasn't long, though, before Kay encountered the phantom visitor for herself.

> It was just a couple of weeks after Bob had seen this guy, when he showed up in front of me. I was doing my housework, just vacuuming the living room. I had the radio turned way up so I could hear it above all the

noise, and everything was normal, just like any other day. Then, when I pulled the vacuum around to do the other side of the room, I saw this pair of legs standing over in the corner, the same corner where Bob had seen this guy. I just froze in my tracks and stared at it. I couldn't believe it. Then, really slow like, the rest of him started to show up. After a few seconds I could see him plain as day, an old man standing there looking back at me. He never moved an inch. Even though he was looking straight at me, he never made a move. The look on his face made me think he was afraid of me, but believe me it was the other way around. I reached down to shut off the vacuum, and when I looked back, he was gone. That's when I headed out the back door and went over to my neighbor's house until Bob got home.

Bob and Kay are good parents, and good parents tend to protect their children from harm. Therefore, they decided against telling the kids about the old man, hoping they'd never see him and all would be as normal as normal can be with an uninvited guest in your house. It wasn't long, though, before the kids began to catch on that something wasn't right in their comfortable, old house.

"We rented a movie," says Kay,

and all of us were in the living room watching it and eating chips and drinking pop. It was some comedy—a Disney movie or something—and we didn't sense anything unusual around us. Then all of a sudden every cabinet door in the kitchen started to slam. It sounded like someone was opening them all up and banging them shut as hard as he could. Bob jumped up to run in there, but he didn't get halfway across the living room when it stopped.

This was only the beginning of the nightly racket coming from the kitchen. Nearly every night, usually between 10 and 10:30, it would sound like someone was rummaging around in the kitchen, going through the cupboards and banging around on the counters. Bob says:

> It wasn't as loud as the first time, but just about the same time every night it sounded like someone was looking around in the kitchen for something. After a few nights of this, I decided to sit in there from about 9:30 to 10:30, hoping I'd see for myself what was going on. But if I was in there, nothing would happen.

Eventually, the kitchen seemed to quiet down, with strange happenings taking place only a couple of times a week. But as the kitchen became quieter, new occurrences began to permeate the house. "Pretty soon, things would come up missing," says Kay.

> Some of my makeup would be gone from my dresser, and some cheap earrings disappeared. Some of this happened to the kids, too. They would complain that their house keys or other little things wouldn't be where they left them. Usually, all this stuff would show up in another part of the house after a while.

Curious as to who their new houseguest might be, the Erwins began to make inquiries about their house. They visited the county courthouse to check the deed and made attempts to contact former owners. In the end they just came up blank. Even the neighbors, in whom they eventually confided, hadn't a clue as to the origins of their haunting. In the meantime, the strange events intermittently continued.

"One night," relates Kay,

> I woke up from a dead sleep in a cold sweat. For some reason I had the overwhelming urge to go downstairs. I knew that if I went down there, I would see this old man again, but I couldn't shake the feeling that I had to go. Part of me felt like if I went down there and he wasn't there, I'd never have to act on another premonition again. I just told myself to be brave and made up my mind to go.

Kay slipped out of bed, tossed on a robe, and headed down the stairs, heart racing and eyes wide with fear. As she passed into the living room, she began to hear the familiar noises of someone rustling through the cupboards. Convinced the old man was rummaging around in there, she quietly sneaked toward the kitchen doorway. Believing she was out of view of the strange old man, she got the scare of her life when she suddenly realized he was standing next to her, quietly observing her from his favorite corner. The scream she let out raised the family from its slumber and effectively erased the ghost from his corner of the living room. It seemed clear to both Bob and Kay that whoever was banging around in the kitchen was not the same man who enjoyed standing rigid in the corner of the living room.

As a curious author, I jumped at the opportunity to spend an evening with the Erwins. Armed with my notebook, tape recorder, camera, and courage, we chatted away in their living room, mixing small talk with ghost talk. Arrangements had been made for the children to stay with their grandparents for the night, so we supposed we had the place as much to ourselves as possible when ghosts are around. I must admit a part of me couldn't wait for the mysterious man in the corner to appear, but a larger part of me would forgive him if he decided to forego his invitation.

As the evening hours drained away, it looked as though the night was going to be a quiet one. Then, about half past ten, the noises began in the kitchen. Sure enough, it sounded as though someone were rifling through the cupboards in search of something. I switched on my recorder, and together the three of us sat in silence and listened to this nocturnal display of rude intrusion. When it quieted down, I rewound my recorder to verify what we had all heard. The tape was blank.

After my visit, the house returned to its normal haunted self. Personal items continued to vanish, sometimes to turn up in another part of the house and sometimes never to be found again. As for the man in the corner, his visits continued until finally the kids caught sight of him. "Our daughter wanted to have some friends over for a sleep-over," says Kay.

> We were apprehensive about it, but decided we couldn't take away her fun just because the place was acting strange. At first, everything was going really well. The girls were all having fun, listening to music and playing video games. I was in the kitchen getting their pizza ready when I heard one of the girls ask our daughter if that was her grandfather she saw standing in the corner. My heart just stopped in my chest. I thought for sure we were going to have a major problem here. But my daughter just shrugged it off and nothing more was said until the next day. That's when she came to me and told me that this old man kept showing up in the living room, watching them. I guess several of the girls caught glimpses of him, but oddly enough they passed it off as one of our relatives.

Desirous of ridding their home of the man in the corner, Bob and Kay picked up several books dealing

Many have seen "the old man in the corner" in this Ludington living room, including children at a sleep-over.

with ghosts and the realm of the paranormal. One of them suggested an old Indian way of keeping spirits at bay—burning sage in the corners of every room, as well as in the entryways and around the windows. They followed these instructions, only to be awakened later that night by the most severe kitchen cabinet pounding to date. "We decided," says Bob, "that our ghosts don't much care for sage and that we weren't going to take any more hints from any books."

As of this writing, the haunting of the Erwin house continues. Bob and Kay insist no old man and no slamming cabinet doors will run them out of their own home. "It gets quieter for a bit," says Bob, "and then seems to pick up again. Right now it's quiet, and maybe it might just go away, but I doubt it."

20

Spectral Sewing Circle

Place Visited: An ornate and expansive two-story home, Victorian in architectural style, located in a historic neighborhood in the city of Marshall, Michigan

Period of Haunting: 1989-present. The current owners suspect that their haunting began many decades past.

Date of Investigation: April, 1998

Description of Location: Marshall is located on the I-94 corridor linking Detroit with Chicago. A highly desirable place to live, Marshall is somewhat upscale and offers a yearly tour of historical homes, an event well-attended by folks from all over the area. The city is nearly a suburb of Battle Creek, and is located about 1-½ hours west of Detroit, in Calhoun County, in the south central portion of the state. The downtown area hosts an array of specialty shops, and one end of the main thoroughfare boasts a beautiful fountain. Marshall is home to the original Win Schuler's Restaurant, a truly class act as far as enchanted and fine dining is concerned. While I could point to many specific areas of interest in this charming city, I cannot point you to the exact location of the home in question, other than to say it is a couple of blocks north of the above-mentioned fountain. Though eager to share their story, the residents of this home treasure their privacy.

The Haunt Meter: * * * *

Kirk and Jean Edmonds purchased this spacious Victorian home immediately after attending its first show-ing. The manicured lawns, the hand-carved staircase, the ornate wood trim, and dozens of other niceties of an era long past seemed to reach out to their hearts and pocketbooks. Children in tow, they quickly made the high bid necessary for a home located in this coveted Marshall neighborhood and moved in with great excite-ment.

"The home was so well maintained," says Kirk, "that there was literally nothing we needed to do to prepare it for our family. Even the carpeting and gilded wallpaper were to our liking."

Kirk and Jean, a white-collar couple with a substan-tial income that can maintain the dignity their home demands, insist the home fits their family like a velvet glove. "Our home is a wonderful haven from the hectic work we do," says Jean.

> We can't wait to get home and shed the layers of frustration we accumulate all day long. Stepping through the front door and into the foyer seems to transport us back in time, to when life was more relaxed and appreciated. That's why we were pleased when we discovered we weren't alone in our home, that a part of that relaxed history of a bygone era has lingered behind.

According to the Edmondses, the haunting first manifested itself in the form of hushed whispers drifting up the staircase from the sitting room below. Jean says:

> Just off the foyer is a large, brightly lighted area that was intended as a sitting room in years past. We've pretty much maintained the integrity of the room, defiling it only with the presence of a television set. Well, one night I had gotten up from bed to visit the bathroom, and as I stepped out into the upstairs hallway, I noticed a light was on down in the sitting room. Thinking one of the kids had forgotten to switch it off, I started down the stairway. About halfway down I began to hear what sounded like women's voices

floating out of that room and up the stairs to where I was standing. I couldn't make out all that was being said, just a few scattered words here and there. I was fascinated by it all, and I tiptoed down the stairs to have a better listen. When I got to about the bottom of the staircase, the talking abruptly stopped. I peeked in the room, and of course no one was there. I turned the light out and went back up to bed.

Jean says she didn't mention this to anyone, as it was an isolated incident, and she wanted to wait and see if anyone else in the family would notice strange happenings in their new home. She didn't have long to wait. Son Jonathan, at the time a high school junior, was next in line to encounter the ghostly voices.

I started a job at McDonald's, and sometimes I'd get home a little past 11 P.M.. Usually, everybody else was already in bed or was awake upstairs waiting for me to get home. I remember the first night I heard the voices. I came in through the back door and walked through the kitchen and the living room to go upstairs to bed. As I got near the stairs, I noticed a light was on in the sitting room. I figured Mom or Dad were in there watching television, but the sounds I heard weren't from the TV. It sounded like a whole bunch of women gabbing away at once. I went in to see who was over, but the instant I stepped into the room the talking all stopped. It really felt spooky, so I hurried upstairs to see if Mom or Dad were awake. When I told them what I'd heard, Dad told me my imagination was running a little overtime, but Mom didn't say anything. It wasn't until the next morning that she let me know she had heard it once before, too.

The gaggle of girls continued with its intermittent chattering in the weeks to come. Even the neighbors began to mention to the Edmonds family how they must be night owls, as the light in that room would be seen burning long after the most valiant of insomniacs would have gone to bed. "It was interesting," says Jean, "how, if any of us got up in the night, the light in that room would almost invariably be burning. Yet in the morning it would be off again."

It never ceases to amaze me how accepting people can be of the ghosts in their home. The Edmondses, not unlike so many other families I've interviewed, soon made the ghostly voices a part of their family. Jean says:

> It very quickly reached a point where it all seemed quite natural. We'd see the lights and hear the voices, and sometimes we'd go down and shut off the lights and sometimes we'd let them continue on with whatever it was they were doing down there.

While the family speculated about the origins of their haunting, the haunting itself seemed limited to the sitting room, and the manifestations remained within the bounds of auditory expression—until the spring of 1998. "It's interesting," muses Kirk,

> that I would be the first one to actually see a ghost in this house. I was the only one who'd never heard the voices. As for the light, I could explain that as someone's forgetfulness. I always said I wouldn't believe in ghosts until one crept up behind me and bit me on the backside. Well, that didn't happen, but the next closest thing to it did.

Kirk was up late one night, laboriously poring over stacks of paperwork related to his job.

> I was at the dining room table, punching numbers into my calculator, long after everyone else had turned in for the night. It was a project I really wanted to get out of the way, so I was still at it past midnight. I remember I got up to go to the kitchen for another in a long line of coffee runs, and when I came back into the dining room I could see the glow of a light drifting through the foyer. Right away I remembered the stories the rest of the family had told about the lights and the voices—interesting how your memory takes on a life of its own after midnight—so I sort of sneaked across the dining room and toward the sitting room. About the time I got to the foyer I saw something I never in my

life thought I'd see. Crossing the foyer in front of me was this beautiful, middle-aged blonde woman. She was dressed in clothing I can only guess to be from the early part of this century, a white blouse with billowy sleeves and a high, lace collar. She also had a long, dark skirt and pointy, black shoes. I remember she had a cameo around her neck, suspended by a ribbon instead of a chain, and she was carrying what appeared to be a silver platter. On the platter were a glass pitcher and some small glass cups. The impression I got was that she was on her way to serve lemonade or something to her guests. As I just stood there on the edge of the foyer, she spirited by me, giving me a bright, friendly smile as she disappeared into the sitting room. I don't recall having heard any voices, and when I went into the sitting room, she was gone. No one was there.

It was about this time that Kirk and Jean decided to give one of Jean's friends a call. Her name is Susanna, and she claims to exhibit psychic tendencies.

I've known Kirk and Jean for years, and Jean always believed in the reality of psychic phenomena. Kirk was always a self-proclaimed skeptic. So when I realized Kirk was in agreement with my coming over for a visit, I knew something must be going on there. When I drove up to the house, I parked on the street and went directly up to the front door. It was dark out, and I could see several lights were on in the house. When I got up to the porch, I saw the curtains in the room to the left of me part, and I got the distinct image in my mind's eye of this beautiful woman in a long, Victorian gown. She was standing at the window, looking out and smiling at me, like she was glad I was there. It turned out to be the same woman Kirk would tell me about seeing.

Susanna did a thorough walk-through of the house, checking out all the rooms for psychic energy. Surprisingly, the house was bereft of any spiritual presence, except in the area of the foyer and sitting room. "The haunting was confined to the foyer and the room to the left of the staircase," asserts Susanna.

> Only in those two areas did I sense the presence of entities. The strongest presence was that of the woman I saw when I was on the porch. The impression I got was that she had lived there years ago, and that she had loved the place dearly and had hosted frequent gatherings of female friends. Inside the sitting room, I sensed the presence of several women and even got a glimpse of a couple of them. They were all there to socialize, to drink tea and work on some sort of project, like sewing or quiltmaking. Everyone was happy and the feeling was really warm and comfortable.

While the spirits were pleased and comfortable with their surroundings, Kirk was not pleased and comfortable with them.

> There's something about seeing ghosts in your house that sort of unsettles you after a while. I knew the rest of the family didn't have a problem with any of this, and that they even found it interesting. But I didn't want to see any ghosts anymore, so I asked Susanna to do something about it. We finally decided that she should tell them they could remain in the house, but that they weren't to disturb us or show themselves to us in any way. So Susanna went into a trance of some sort and conveyed my wishes. Since then, we haven't encountered much of anything.

The haunting of this Marshall home has quieted considerably. While the family is certain their ghosts are still in residence, only infrequently can a light be seen casting its eerie glow across the threshold of the sitting room and into the foyer. As for the lady with the lemonade, she appears to have slipped into the shadows herself. "I think I overdid it," admits Kirk. "We all miss the mystery and excitement of sharing our home with guests from another dimension. I've played with the idea of having Susanna return and invite them all back again. Besides," he says with a twinkle in his eye, "she was a pretty good-looking lady."

21

Demon in the Dark

Place Visited: A two-story, single-residence home, dating back to the early 1930s, in Milford, Michigan

Period of Haunting: Fall, 1989

Date of Investigation: February, 2000. Due to the circumstances indicated below, I did no more than drive past this house and interview the main character in our tale.

Description of Location: Milford is an upscale community, with a delightful and eclectic downtown spotted with shops and restaurants sure to satisfy your curiosity as well as your hunger pangs. Primarily a bedroom community for those who draw their bonus checks from suburban Detroit business and industry, it is a high-rent area, with prime real estate commanding premium prices. Though growing quickly and coveted as a prestigious place to live, it is still surrounded by great, open areas of natural beauty. You may reach Milford by following either US-23 or I-75 northward and exiting at M-59. Milford lies between these expressways, slightly to the south of M-59. Since this story deals with ex-spouses, the author determined it wise to leave the exact location of the house a mystery. However, it is within walking distance of Appeteasers, a charming restaurant with cuisine (ask about their entree of chicken livers with strawberry sauce) and service to match.

The Haunt Meter: * * * *

Harry was trying to survive what was quite possibly the most traumatic event of his life. His wife, whom he would divorce in the near future, was abusing drugs and alcohol. Her habit went beyond occasional recreational use, and she was finding, shall we say, creative ways to feed her habit. For his part, Harry had tried almost every intervention available and was hanging on to the frayed ends of the proverbial rope by his fingernails.

Harry recalls how one night he confronted his wife with her errant ways, spelling out the disastrous direction their relationship was headed if she continued to refuse help. For the first time in months, she actually began to break down and share her horror with him.

> It was really pitiful to watch. Her eyes were distant and her skin was sallow. She had lost a great deal of weight, and it was clear she was totally exhausted. But even so, she refused to let go of her addiction. I spoke to her about how the drugs would most likely kill her someday, but she was too hooked to give them up. She did, however, open up and begin to tell me about a recurring vision she would have, in which she could see down into what she called the "sewers of hell" and a shrouded, demonic figure would appear to her. She said she would see it more and more as her drug usage escalated. She was terrified of it but felt powerless to make it go away.

As they sat in the living room of their home, sharing a last, lost conversation, Harry began to sense a change in the room itself. It grew shadowy, as though a gray pall had descended upon them. Perhaps it's best at this point to let Harry, an articulate and well-educated professional man, describe what happened next.

> My ex was seated on the living room sofa, and I was seated across the room from her in my recliner. Between us and off to my right was the doorway leading outside. To my left, and next to the sofa, turned at an angle where she could not see it, was the television set.

As she spoke of her nightmarish visions, the room began to darken. I remember my skin beginning to tingle, like some sort of low-level electrical charge was passing by me. Then, as she continued to speak in an almost trance-like state, I saw the reflection of some sort of entity begin to slowly spread across the glass of the darkened television screen.

All I saw was the reflection of the entity, not the entity itself. The face was featureless, shrouded in shadow by a hood it wore. Only the eyes were distinguishable. The eyes were yellow and set wide apart and very hypnotic in nature. The more my ex detailed her nightly descent into the sewers of her drug-induced dreams, the more clear the apparition appeared on the screen. From her vantage point, she was not able to see the reflection, although she may have been able to see it directly, which I could not. At one point, I moved up in my chair to wave my hand in front of the television, to see if my hand could be reflected on the screen. It could not. Furthermore, my hand did not interfere in any way with the reflection of this demonic figure.

The eyes were its method of communication. As I sat transfixed by them, the glimpse of evil, death, terror, sickness, and doom was horrifying. Yet I could not turn away from it. The question yet unresolved for me is, was I looking at its soul, at her soul, or my own soul? After the reflection left, she described this shrouded demon as the central character in her vision. I felt as though her living hell was soon to envelop me as well.

Not long after this demonic encounter, Harry left his wife and filed for divorce. He maintains he has never been so frightened of losing his soul as he was on that singular evening in Milford. He simply cannot comprehend anyone slipping as deeply into the bowels of self-destruction and evil as his wife had. To this day, the memory of that horrific night still spawns nightmares that interrupt his sleep.

Harry's ex-wife still resides in the home they once

shared. Harry has had no contact with her to determine if the demonic figure is still present in her life.

22

Amish Kids Like Cake, Too

Place Visited: An old, two-story farmhouse just inside the northern village limits of Montgomery, Michigan

Period of Haunting: 1982-present

Date of Investigation: July, 1999

Description of Location: Montgomery is a very small village tucked away in the southernmost portion of Hillsdale County near the tri-state borders where Michigan, Indiana, and Ohio meet. Take M-99 south from US-12 past beautiful rolling hills and lush farmland and follow the signs into the village.

The Haunt Meter: * * * *

Greg and Peggy Hess (not their real names) were pleased to find an empty farmhouse large enough to meet the needs of their young and growing family. Having five active children and only the modest income Greg earned as a Hillsdale County sheriff's deputy to support them, this old, two-story, wood-frame house met the Hess's familial and financial needs quite well.

"It was a drafty old house," says Greg, a large man with an outgoing personality, "and the wind would literally blow through some of the hairline cracks in the walls, especially upstairs where the kids slept. I don't think there was a level floor in the house, and there was this damp Michigan basement that reminded us of something out of an old horror movie." Basically, a Michigan basement is an unimproved, sub-level storage area with dirt floors and usually no windows. In years past they were popular as cool places to store fruits and vegetables.

Montgomery is a small village, populated mostly by farmers and those who drive into the cities of Hillsdale or Adrian for employment. It is in the heart of Michigan's Amish country, and just across the border in Indiana there is a quite large and prosperous Amish community. Herein lies the gist of our tale.

"I remember I came home from my afternoon shift," recalls Greg, "and Peggy told me I needed to talk to my youngest daughter, Jackie, that she was really upset about something that had happened to her earlier that evening. So I went up to her room—it must have been around 11:30—to check on her, and she was still awake, and I could tell she was still really scared."

Jackie told her father that, earlier that evening, while playing hide-and-seek with her siblings and some neighbor kids, she had decided to find a good hiding spot down in the basement. She knew it would be a great place to hide because her brothers and sisters were all afraid to go down there. She went on to say that she crept down the stairs and, using a flashlight because there was no electricity down there, found a stack of old, wooden crates to hide behind. After only a few moments of hiding, one of the other kids opened the door at the top of the stairs, which allowed a splinter of light to pierce the blackness. At that point Jackie saw a little boy, about ten years old, standing in the corner of the basement opposite her. He was dressed in black pants and a black coat, with what appeared to be a blue shirt and a round, black hat. For only a few seconds he was perfectly illuminated by the light from above. Then, said Jackie, the door closed and she couldn't see him any more.

"As she told me her story," says Greg, "I could see

she was still trembling all over. My wife said she heard her screaming down there and had to go down and bring her back upstairs. Later, after making sure Jackie fell asleep OK, I went down there with my service flashlight, but of course I didn't find anything."

It wasn't long before the haunting picked up a bit. "I remember lots of times," recalls Peggy, "when I would go into the kitchen and there would be the powerful smell of freshly-baked bread. It would hang in the air for several minutes, and then it would suddenly just go away. Sometimes the kids would smell it, too." The kitchen seemed to be a focal point for this activity. "There were many times," continues Peggy, "when I'd be fixing supper and out of the corner of my eye I would see someone pass by the kitchen doorway—I could never tell if it was a man or a woman, but it was definitely an adult, a tall, black image that moved very quickly."

It seems the old Montgomery farmhouse is host to more than just a couple of spirits. Greg recalls the afternoon he returned home from work, and Peggy and the kids had all gone into Jackson to shop.

> The house was empty, and it was a beautiful summer's day, so Peggy left some of the windows open. I changed out of my uniform, fixed myself a sandwich, and went into the living room to watch TV. After a few minutes of relaxing in front of the tube, I could hear children playing in the backyard. It sounded like several kids, all running around and laughing and having a great time. For a minute I thought Peggy and the kids had come home, but when I got up to look, the sound stopped and there was nobody in the yard. I went back to watching my flick, and pretty soon it all started up again, the sound of kids laughing and playing.

Intrigued by the phantom voices of playful children, Greg decided to sit out on the back porch, just outside the kitchen, and listen for their return.

> I thought maybe they'd start up again in the backyard, so I took a chair from the kitchen and sat on the porch.

Only this time, the noise seemed to be coming from inside the house. It was just like there were several kids running through the house and yelling, like they were having a great time. So, I stepped back through the porch door and into the kitchen, and immediately the noises stopped. It was more than a little spooky.

It wasn't long before Greg and Peggy finally got an up-close-and-personal look at at least one of the spectres in their home. "It was late at night," remembers Peggy,

and the kids were all asleep. I stayed up waiting for Greg to get home, which was well after midnight. We had a snack and then went to bed. No sooner had we turned off the lamp on the nightstand, when we both saw a middle-aged woman, dressed in the clothes the Amish would wear, walk into our bedroom. She was carrying a candle, which lit up her face pretty well. She seemed pleasant looking, and she wore a white, cap-like bonnet on her head. She was as solid and real looking as any living person I had ever seen. She walked into our bedroom, smiled at us, then turned and literally walked through the bedroom wall and disappeared. At first it seemed perfectly normal, but then, after a minute or two, I was scared as hell.

With five young children in the house, it's got to be hard to tell when a extra spirit or two is around. So, whenever the kids would complain about misplaced toys or lights left on that they thought they had turned off, Greg and Peggy didn't know whom to blame, the kids in this dimension or the ones in the next. But there was at least one incident in which Peggy knew it wasn't her kids being mischievous.

Greg was working an afternoon shift, and wasn't due home until after midnight. I had put the kids down by 9:30 because it was a school night. Then I went into the kitchen and decided to make a cake for the next day—basically just something to do to kill time until Greg got home. Well, I finished the cake and left it on the counter to cool. I figured I could frost it the next day. I went into the living room to watch television, and after a while I must have dozed off. I remember being woken up by the sound of kids talking in the kitchen. I figured some of my kids had sneaked downstairs and were raiding the refrigerator while Mom slept in front of the television.

It appears this wasn't the case.

I went into the kitchen, all set to read the kids the riot act and send them back to bed. But the instant I flicked on the kitchen light, the voices stopped. I looked around the kitchen—it's fairly large—and there was no one there. As if that weren't weird enough, my cake was half eaten—it hadn't been cut into pieces; it was like someone had torn off hunks of it with their bare hands. There were crumbs all over the counter and a pile of crumbs on the floor. That's when I turned all the lights in the house on and waited for Greg to come home.

The Hesses continued to live in the house for the next couple of years. During that time, they continued to encounter fleeting glimpses of Amish children, and the usual potpourri of paranormal activity abounded—doors opening by themselves, lights switching on and off, and the sound of kids playing when no kids were around. The activity became somewhat normal to them, right up until the day they moved away, into a more modern home near the city of Hillsdale. "The last day there," remembers Greg, "we all stood in the front yard and said our good-byes to whomever was in the house, and then we drove away. I've got to believe that if it was that haunted then, it has to be haunted still today."

As a final note, I had the opportunity to visit the Hess family during the time of their haunting. If the house wasn't haunted, it sure looked like it should have been. I've not had the opportunity to speak with the new residents in order to confirm or deny any current ghostly activity.

23

A Piano, a Water Bucket, and Fingers under the Door

Place Visited: A large, two-story home in a rather cramped neighborhood near the campus of Central Michigan University in Mt. Pleasant, Michigan

Period of Haunting: 1996-present

Date of Investigation: October, 1998

Description of Location: Mt. Pleasant is a college town in every sense of the word. The town is home to Central Michigan University, a huge and diverse bastion of higher education, and offers something for just about every taste. If gambling is your game, you can check out the Soaring Eagle Casino, about one mile east of town; or if your taste buds cry out, try the Mountain Town Station, a former train station converted into an eatery and mini-brewery that offers some truly great barbecued ribs and home-brewed lagers. Mt. Pleasant is located smack dab in the middle of Michigan's Lower Peninsula. From the Detroit area, take I-96 west to Lansing and continue north on US-27. Get off at the first Mt. Pleasant exit, which spills you directly onto one of the city's main thoroughfares. Go to Bellows Street and turn left at the light. Continue to north Fancher and turn right. Somewhere up the street is the haunted house.

The Haunt Meter: * * * * *

This haunted house lies just north of the campus of Central Michigan University. Many of the homes in this area are old and in great need of periodic repairs, not only due to age, but also because many of these structures have been converted into apartments to meet the housing demands of a huge student body.

Curtis Sanborn (not his real name) purchased this old, two-story, wood-frame home for investment purposes. It was a large and imposing structure, and Curtis knew that with a few modifications it would make a great place to house college students. He realized the extent of work needed to bring the place up to code, but with his savings, and perhaps a few loans from family members, he knew he could whip it into shape before the start of the fall semester.

Renovations were a bit more extensive than otherwise planned, and Curtis found himself enmeshed in repair work. A carpenter by trade, he decided the best thing to do would be to move into the old place for a few weeks so he wouldn't have to lug his tools and equipment back and forth every day.

In the course of tearing out the old upstairs bathroom fixtures, Curtis discovered that the pipes were susceptible to breaks and found it necessary to shut down the water supply for a few days until repairs could be made. For drinking water, he brought in a few cases of bottled water. For flushing purposes on the main floor, where the pipes were still intact, he kept two five-gallon pails of water on the kitchen counters.

"The first strange thing I noticed," says Curtis,

had to do with those water buckets. One afternoon after work, I was in the kitchen getting a beer from the refrigerator. I heard water splashing behind me, but I knew that couldn't be possible because the water main was shut off. I turned around to look, and one of the pails of water was splashing around, like it would be if someone put their hand in it and started slapping the water around. Just the one bucket was doing it. The other bucket, sitting right next to it, wasn't moving at all; it was perfectly still. I stood there drinking my beer and watching it for about three or four minutes, and then it stopped. It couldn't have been a vibration from outside causing it, because just the one bucket was splashing around.

Curtis is a rather macho fellow, not given to fear and trembling. Although he had felt there was something strange about the place the day he first looked it over, no ghost and no water bucket shenanigans were going to get in his way of converting the old place into a money-making venture. Ignoring the water bucket, he continued with his work.

The first weekend Curtis spent in the house was dedicated to making the upstairs bathroom functional. He arose early on Saturday morning, breakfasted at a local eatery, and dove into his work, pulling out pipes, ripping the old sink off the wall, and dragging out the tired, old bathtub.

I'd been working for several hours and all the way through lunch. I had opened the window up there so I could throw out broken pipes and scrap material down into the backyard. Since it was kind of cool outside and the window was open, I had the bathroom door closed so the furnace wouldn't run too much. I was working away and, out of the corner of my eye, I saw something moving around underneath the bathroom door. At first I thought it was a mouse, but when I turned and looked at it, it was fingers. I could see fingers sliding underneath the door, wiggling around like they were trying to feel for something. I figured one of my buddies had come in and was pranking me, but when I opened the door there wasn't anyone there. Now I have to admit, that sort of scared the snot out of me. I ran downstairs to see if anyone had come over, but the house was empty and the doors were still locked up. I went back upstairs to finish my work, and all day long I kept glancing over at the door, but I didn't see anything more that day. I did get the strong sense I wasn't alone in there, though.

As if the water bucket incident and the fingers under the doorway weren't enough, Curtis soon encountered yet another strange phenomenon. When he bought the place, he had inherited a piano that the former owners no longer wanted. It was just an old piano, probably worth more as kindling than as entertainment. "It was basically junk," says Curtis. "My plans were to haul it away or give it away, whichever opportunity arose first. Some of the keys didn't even work anymore, and it was in pretty knocked-up shape."

Curtis arrived at his new investment home very late one night, after treating a few of his co-workers to beers at one of the local watering holes. Tired and slightly under the influence of black-and-tan, he headed immediately to bed, stretching himself out on the cot he kept in the downstairs dining room.

> I don't think I had even fallen asleep yet, when I heard someone plinking away on that old crap piano. It wasn't any song they were playing—it just sounded like someone using one finger at a time and randomly hitting some keys. It wasn't very loud, but at 1 A.M. any piano playing is bound to get your attention, especially if you're supposed to be in the house alone.

Raising himself off the cot, Curtis grabbed a pipe wrench out of his toolbox and headed toward the living room, where the piano was located. Peering into the darkness, he could make out the image of the piano, and he could hear a few notes being tapped out, presumably by someone. Not a soul, however, could be seen anywhere.

> I listened to it for a few seconds, and then I switched on the light. When I did, it stopped. I searched the house, although I knew I was alone, and all was in order. I went back to bed, and the music started up again. This nonsense continued off and on through the night, and each time I got up to check it out, it stopped. Eventually I just went to sleep.

Curtis continued with his renovations, completing the upstairs bathroom and updating some of the bedrooms as well. After several weeks, the house was nearing a condition in which he could take satisfaction, and all that was left was to add new outlet boxes in some of the bedrooms.

"I took my girlfriend out for dinner one night," recalls Curtis.

We pretty much closed the place up, and instead of taking her home, she decided to stay the night at my new place, since the next day was Saturday and she had offered to help me with the electrical work. When we got there, she headed upstairs to use the bathroom, since it was newly remodeled and in better shape than the one downstairs. I had the power shut off because of the electrical work I had been doing, so while she went upstairs, I went down to the basement to turn the power back on. About the time I got to the breaker box, I heard her scream, and I shot back up the stairs to the bathroom. She was absolutely terrified when I got there.

It seems that Curtis's girlfriend, who prefers anonymity, had no sooner got in the bathroom than she heard scratching noises on the door. Armed with a flashlight until Curtis would turn on the lights, she had directed her beam at the base of the door. She was less than pleasantly entertained by the sight of someone's fingers protruding under the doorway, scratching the wood with its fingernails. Although Curtis turned the power on and inspected the house, she nonetheless decided to return home.

Curtis has no clues to the tormentor in his new home. Undeterred by the strange events, he continued with his fix-up job and had no problem finding tenants from the nearby university.

I keep thinking, that I'm going to get some phone calls soon from some of the guys and girls living there, telling me about the ghosts, but so far there hasn't been a peep. I think that whoever is haunting the place—and there may be more than one—is probably still pulling pranks. I think it just doesn't get noticed because of all the activity in the house. There are always a lot of people in and out of the place, and there seems to be parties going on quite a bit. With all that activity, I imagine the ghosts don't get noticed.

According to Curtis, the home is probably still haunted. He hasn't had the opportunity to spend much time there other than to make small repairs as needed. Even then he senses nothing out of the ordinary. His girlfriend, however, still refuses to enter the place.

24

Staying after School

Place Visited: Pinconning High School, Pinconning, Michigan

Period of Haunting: Of unknown duration. Legend claims that the haunting goes back decades. The experiences herein cover the period 1995-1999.

Date of Investigation: Fall, 1998

Description of Location: Pinconning is a pleasant and relaxed small town of about 1,300 living souls, about 15 miles north of Bay City. Many people know this city because of the cheese that once carried its name. It now relies heavily upon the tourists who pass through town on their way north, heading for hunting camps in the winter, and the azure lakes and streams in the summer. If passing through Pinconning, make it a point to pause at Purtell's, a family-owned restaurant and dairy, which serves wonderful ice cream concoctions. I recommend the Kitchen Sink, several flavors smothered in a variety of toppings and served in, you guessed it, a kitchen sink—enough to feed a small family. From the south, reach the town by taking either I-75 to the Pinconning exit and heading east two miles, at which point you will find the school immediately on your right. Alternatively, motor north on M-13 from Bay City, a route that will deliver you directly through the heart of town. Pinconning High School is one block west of the intersection of M-13 and Pinconning Road. It is an old, sprawling, one-story building that some locals insist is in dire need of replacement or restoration.

The Haunt Meter: * * *

During the daylight hours, Pinconning High School is as active and noisy as any school you can imagine. Shouting voices, shuffling feet hurrying to classrooms, and the banging of locker doors fill the air. In this respect, it differs in no way from any other school packed with pupils. Maybe because of this, most of the paranormal activity reported to exist within its walls occurs after hours, when the halls have hushed and the doors have been bolted.

Bob Coleman is a custodian with the Pinconning Area School District. Having enough seniority to select his shift, it isn't surprising that he chose the afternoon shift at the high school. After all, the school is literally in his backyard, allowing him to take his lunch breaks with his family. This later shift also affords Bob the opportunity to confront a few students who have long since exited the building, if not this earthly plane.

"I'm not the only one who knows something strange is going on in there," says Bob. "Others I've worked with have noticed stuff, too." Bob, a straightforward kind of guy who loves living near his favorite hunting and fishing spots, is not the sort of man who spooks easily. "I've been stranded out on the ice on Saginaw Bay and rescued from a floe by the Coast Guard, plus I've been turned around a bit after dark in the woods while hunting, but even all that never gave me goose bumps like what goes on in the school," he says.

Bob tells of pulling afternoon shifts when just he and one other custodian, working on opposite ends of the school, were in the building. Bob's duties included cleaning classrooms and vacuuming hallways near the gymnasium.

> I'd be working away, just minding my own business, and all of a sudden I'd hear all kinds of voices coming from out of the gym, just like there was a basketball game or something going on, it would be that loud. You'd swear there were kids cheering and yelling and having a good time, but if I stepped into the gym, it

would just all stop.

Bob is careful to specify, "IF I stepped into the gym," because it reached a point where the talking and laughing got on his nerves. "After a while, I didn't want to hear this stuff any more," says Bob, "so I'd put my radio headphones on and listen to music while I worked. Sometimes it was the best way to distract myself."

Bob isn't the only one to encounter strange occurrences within these venerated halls of secondary education. A cook at the school would often relate to others that certain electrical outlets would inexplicably shut off, prompting her to find alternate ways to heat the students' lunches. After lunch ended, the outlets would work perfectly. This also happened to others in the building. Dave (name changed at his request) is a local citizen who enjoys helping out the drama club when it performs the yearly musicals for which Pinconning High School is locally famous.

> I'd go in some afternoons after school had let out and fix some chow for the cast and crew, since they couldn't get home for supper. I'd plug in my roasters to heat their meal, and the plugs wouldn't work. I'd have to haul my stuff over to another part of the dining area and start over. The strange thing is that none of the breakers were ever popped, and after I didn't need those outlets anymore, they'd work just fine. I could even heat up the leftovers.

Pinconning High School, home to active students during the day and active sprits at nights.

As an interested author, I spent some time interviewing several folks who claimed the premises were haunted. Sure enough, I ran across plenty of parents and students who have had peculiar brushes of their own. Many profess to have experienced strange lights switching off, doors closing, and the occasional array of voices spilling out of the gym and into the halls—all apparently by disembodied types. At least one parent told of driving past the school at night, when even the custodians were clear of the place, and seeing soft lights floating about between the main entry and the gym.

Custodian Bob is quick to admit he's not the only one to see and hear things late in the evening when the old building is locked up.

> There's a woman who works part-time with me, and she's got some psychic abilities. She keeps telling me about the stuff she sees and hears—especially about the woman she keeps running into in one of the halls. She says its a lady near her 60s, and that she's carrying a ruler and is dressed the way teachers did a whole lot of years ago. She'll see this woman coming down the halls, and then she turns and disappears into one of the classrooms. I think it's interesting that the hallway she shows up in is the one which displays all the graduating class pictures from about 1915 to 1970. Maybe the old gal still thinks she belongs there, like she's still attached to her old students.

As one who still harbors affectionate memories of his own alma mater, I suppose it's not unusual that Pinconning High holds a special place in the hearts of its students. Even those who have long since departed its hallowed halls.

25

Lady in Distress

Place Visited: A brick, single-story ranch home located on Mackinaw Road about two miles north of Saginaw, Michigan

Period of Haunting: A three-month period during spring, 1998

Date of Investigation: June, 1998

Description of Location: Saginaw is a large city by Saginaw Bay, near the thumb of Michigan's Lower Peninsula. Mackinaw Road runs from the downtown northward through the small city of Pinconning and into the distance beyond. Driving through this area, one is struck by how flat the terrain suddenly becomes. The site of the mystery home is just outside Saginaw and just before the US-20 overpass. The home sits by itself, about 100 feet off the road, with a driveway lined with evergreens.

The Haunt Meter: * * * ½

While serving as an adjunct instructor of English at Saginaw Valley State University, teaching creative writing (fun) and professional and business writing (mundane), I met another adjunct who shared my interest in otherworldly encounters such as haunted homes. Her name is Elise Warthman, which is as fine a fictitious name as I can imagine, and her interest in the paranormal found additional food for thought in an encounter she had over several evenings in the spring of

1998.

Having survived a rather unpleasant divorce (is there really any other kind?), Elise and her teenaged daughter, Marty, rented a house and set up housekeeping in an attempt to begin life anew. The first few months were uneventful, with not a hint of anything "extra-normal," as Elise would describe haunting experiences. In fact, she and her daughter, who are both studious, very much enjoyed the idea that the nearest neighbor was several empty lots away, and seclusion suited them quite well.

As late spring approached, so did the Michigan thaw, which left their driveway, as well as the path up to their front door, decidedly muddy. Anyone who came to call couldn't help but leave messy evidence of their visitation all over the stoop. That's why mother and daughter found it odd that on several evenings their doorbell rang, but upon opening the door, no one could be found, and no muddy telltale signs were apparent.

"There were many nights," says Elise,

> usually just after 10 P.M., when the doorbell would ring, and either my daughter or I would look out the front window to see who was there. We always used this precaution, because we were new to the area, and because we're two women living alone. Invariably, there would be no one at the door. On those occasions when we would then open the front door and look outside, there would be no muddy footprints on the stoop. We thought this to be quite strange and couldn't pass it off as a faulty doorbell, because it never did this any other time of the day, only after 10 P.M. or so.

The ringing of the bell took place for several nights in late May. It soon reached a point where neither Elise nor Marty would even bother to look outside. They just passed it off as a spectral encounter. "Mom and I once lived in a haunted house," explains Marty,

> so this all seemed sort of natural to us. We would hear the bell, look at each other, and just sort of blow it off.

Mom would say something like, "No sweat, it's just the ghost again." A couple of times, just as the bell would ring, we thought we could hear a woman talking to someone out on the porch. But whenever we checked it out, there was no one around.

The doorbell event reached its culmination one evening when Elise was home alone. Marty had gone out for the evening to shop with friends at the nearby Fashion Square Mall. Hearing the doorbell ring shortly after 11 P.M., Elise instinctively thought it must be Marty, that she had forgotten her keys.

Without thinking, I opened the front door to let Marty in, only it wasn't Marty standing on the porch. Instead, there was this middle-aged woman and a young girl. Immediately I was struck by their appearance. They were both rather modestly dressed, in subdued clothing that reflected the styles of the '50s, nothing flashy about them at all, and the woman was quite serene looking, almost expressionless. I remember thinking to myself how awfully pale the both of them appeared. I think I knew right away they weren't from this world, but at the same time I knew I had nothing to be fearful about. The woman was holding the hand of a girl I assumed to be her daughter, a pleasant-looking child of about seven. From the point they entered my living room, everything they did seemed rehearsed and mechanical, as though they had played this scene several times before. The woman calmly looked right into my eyes and said that her car had broken down out on the road, and that she needed to telephone someone for help. So, I invited them further into the house and showed them to the telephone. From the moment I had opened my door to them, there was an uncanny stillness all around me. The night was thick with fog, and I couldn't hear any of the usual outdoor noises— no automobile sounds, no crickets, nothing but stillness.

Elise was, of course, intrigued by the phantom guests who now stood before her in her living room. In particular, she stared intently at the little girl, who was dressed in a long, pink coat and black patent leather shoes. On her head was a pink and gray silk scarf, a fashion statement which had decades ago lost its appeal to young and old women alike. Fascinated by her nocturnal house guests, she offered them no particular privacy, and instead listened intently to the telephone call being placed by this phantom mother.

> She never let go of her daughter's hand. She made her connection and told someone named Daniel that her car had broken down and she needed to be picked up. Not once did she mention where she was, where the car was, or what was the matter with the car. She just said she needed to be picked up, and then hung up the phone.

Although ghosts dialing numbers on your telephone isn't the most common of occurrences, Elise felt no apprehension as the two strange visitors went about their business.

> They were so absolutely detached and emotionless, not at all what a woman would act like if she were broken down on the road late on a foggy night with her child in tow. So, I decided to make the most of it, and asked if they'd like to sit and wait for their help to arrive. That's when this lady slowly turned her head toward me and, calmly but politely, simply said "no," and walked toward the door.

Elise showed her guests to the stoop, and, upon their exit, closed the door behind them. Immediately, she realized the appetite of her fascination required more of this apparitional episode, and so instantly she flung the door open once again.

> There couldn't have been more than two or three seconds between my closing and opening the door, but when I reopened it, they were gone. The fog was so thick I could only see halfway down the drive, but they were nowhere to be seen. Then, when I looked down at the porch, there were no muddy footprints anywhere. At that point, I just went back inside, fixed a cup of

herbal tea, and sat on the couch in total astonishment until Marty returned home from her shopping trip. When she did return, I couldn't wait for her friends to leave so I could share all this with her. And when her friends did leave, I made a point of checking out the porch for muddy footprints, and, of course, her friends had tracked up the cement pretty badly.

Elise and Marty now wonder if this was the woman who had incessantly rung their bell over the past several weeks. One would be safe in surmising that it was, because after this haunting exchange, the ringing of the bell came to a halt. "I believe that any given night on which I would have opened the door when the bell rang," says Elise,

> this woman would have been standing on my porch with her daughter, asking to use the phone. Maybe she was even there on those nights when I had opened the door, but for some reason we just couldn't connect. Perhaps my state of mind was on the wrong wavelength. I believe she kept ringing each night until I let her inside to call for help.

Elise knows no history of the area nor of any local legend about a spectral woman visiting homes in search of help. Although neither she nor her daughter have seen this phantom pair again, there are still moments when, late in the evening when the house is still, they feel they hear the hushed whisperings of a woman outside their front door. "If she's still out there," says Elise, "I hope to heaven we have another chance to see her, and that Marty can witness it all for herself as well."

26

The Lady in the Park

Place Visited: McCourtie Park in Somerset Township, Michigan

Period of Haunting: These events took place in the summers of 1994 and 1995; additional sightings may not be uncommon, as this is a public park.

Date of Investigation: Summer, 1995

Description of Location: McCourtie Park, owned and operated by Somerset Township, is located in Somerset Center, in the northern part of Michigan's lush and scenic Hillsdale County, in the extreme south-central part of the state. Racing enthusiasts will note that Somerset Center is about ten miles west of Michigan International Speedway. The park itself is fairly small,

with a meandering creek and a quaint wooden bridge, as well as several cement trees which dot the landscape, an oddity which only seems to add to the park's attractiveness. The park is adjacent to the north edge of US-12, about four miles west of US-127, just down the road from Bino's Restaurant, a great place for country-style breakfasts where the locals love to gather after worship services on Sunday. Although a beautiful place to relax or enjoy a picnic, McCourtie Park is not in frequent use, as nearby Lake LeAnn and Lake Somerset afford many residents just about all the recreation their hearts desire.

The Haunt Meter: * * ½

This is not a particularly frightening account, as the McCourtie Park ghost appears quite innocuous and is infrequently encountered. I include it simply because I'm convinced it has merit, as it comes from reliable sources.

I first heard of the so called "lady in the shed" from an employee of one of the local businesses in Somerset Center. As I have a summer home at one of the nearby private-lake communities, it's not uncommon for me to frequent these local enterprises, and when I do, I usually find a way to bring up the subject of hauntings. Sheila, a young woman of unusual beauty and gregarious personality, relayed this intriguing tale as I made my usual early evening junk food purchase at her shop.

My boyfriend and I decided to have a picnic in the park one afternoon. We were supposed to be in school, but it was such a nice day we skipped out and took a blanket and some pop and hamburgers and headed over to the park. We listened to music, ate our lunch, and basically soaked up some rays before deciding to take a walk. Since my boyfriend had brought his boom box, he thought he'd better stick it in his trunk instead of leaving it on the grass next to our blanket. So, he headed to the car, on the other side of the park, and I waited for him.

Sheila watched as her boyfriend crossed one of the cement bridges over the meandering creek and disappeared over a grassy knoll and toward the parking area. The sun was warm, and the air filled with the scattered songs of the various birds making flight all around her.

As I stood there, just enjoying the peace and quiet of the afternoon, I began to notice just how pretty the park really is. I was soaking in all this peacefulness, when I noticed someone standing in front of the long, single-story building that's actually built into the side of a hill. That building is divided up into several sections, and I guess the township just uses them all for storage now. It was a small woman and she was really dressed funny. Here it was, a gorgeous, warm spring day, and she had on a long, dark blue dress

The female ghost of McCourtie Park can sometimes be seen entering and exiting this building's center door. Originally a tavern and restaurant, it's built into the side of a hill, hence its roof of grass. The trees above are concrete and hollow, having served as vents for illegal stills during Prohibition.

with sleeves down to her wrists. Her shoes were black, with buttons up the front, and she wore a black bonnet over her upbraided hair. I mean, she really didn't fit the place or the time. My first thought was that there must be some sort of historical presentation taking place in the park, but we were the only ones around.

Sheila says she watched this woman as the woman also seemed to be watching her. It seemed a pleasant enough exchange, as Sheila says the woman smiled at her, casually surveyed the greenery surrounding the meandering creek, and then turned around and went inside one section of that building.

When my boyfriend came back from the car, I told him what I saw. Then we both walked over to where I'd seen her—it was only about 30 yards away—and we checked the place out. No one was around, and all the sections of the building were locked up tight from the outside. We peeked through every window of every section, trying to find out where this lady could have gone, but she had just disappeared. For a long time my boyfriend thought I was pulling a prank on him, but I wasn't, I really saw this woman. I've never seen a ghost before, but that's what she must have been, except ghosts are supposed to scare you, and I wasn't scared at all.

Sheila is not the only one who claims to have seen the lady in blue. A part-time reporter for a local small-town newspaper also tells of visiting the park and encountering an extra-dimensional guest. Linda Strathmore (not her real name) was a writer for the *Brooklyn Exponent*, published in the nearby town of Brooklyn.

I was in the area working on a story and decided to stop off for a few minutes and enjoy the park. It's really a beautiful little park, and it's too bad no one uses it very much. Anyway, I was drinking a Coke and wandering across one of the cute little bridges they have there, when I glanced over at the strange building they have that's carved into the side of a hill, and saw a woman standing near one of the doorways. I knew

One of several such bridges in McCourtie Park built by Mexican artisans in the 1930s. Made of cement, several species of trees are depicted on each structure. Our ghost has been known to cross this particular bridge.

immediately she wasn't from our time, because she was dressed in really old clothing, a style no way near modern fashion standards.

Linda went on to tell of how she observed this lady in a dark blue dress and black bonnet standing by that doorway, seemingly pleased with the surroundings. Then, the woman opened the door behind her and disappeared inside.

I suddenly became very interested in her. I knew this woman didn't belong in our time frame, so I right away headed straight for where I had seen her standing, making a beeline for the door. I remember I wasn't the least bit afraid, this woman seemed so pleasant. But when I got to the door, it was locked up tight. There was no way anyone could have gone inside and at the same time have locked the door from the outside. So I stood there for a while, hoping she would come back outside again, but after an hour or so, I gave up and went home. It wasn't until after I got back home that I began to feel a little weird about it all.

I visited this little park for myself, and it is indeed an odd place. Upon entering, you don't even realize that built into the earth beneath your feet is a long, cement structure, which appears to have been at one time a collection of shops. Peering inside, you can spy pictures on the walls of days gone by. In front of this recessed building are two ancient swimming pools, now surrounded by fences and, though filled with water, obviously no longer in use.

Although it's possible to literally jump across the creek that flows through this park, the water is spanned by several rare and unique foot bridges. The park was once the estate of W.H.L. McCourtie, who made his fortune in the cement business out west and then returned home to Somerset Township to bless the community with his good fortune. He had long admired a form of cement artwork the Mexican artisans of the old west perfected, in which they replicated numerous species of trees with wet cement. A close look at the bridges in McCourtie Park will reveal various grains and textures of trees indigenous to the area.

As if there weren't enough trees already sprouting forth in this pristine portion of lower Michigan, McCourtie also directed his artisans to construct cement trees, which are now scattered across the park's landscape. While he may have been eccentric, McCourtie was a well-loved man in the area and hosted many community events on the grounds, especially during the Depression, when local money was tight. His community shindigs were attended by hundreds, and he provided all the music and food with funds from his own fortune. Upon his death, the farmstead went into a state of disrepair until the township purchased it several years ago and restored it to a portion of its former beauty.

An interesting side note to this story concerns a few of those cement trees the Mexican artists designed. A couple of those trees rest atop the hill under which that long row of shops is built. It seems those two trees are hollow and were actually designed as chimneys for the underground building. As many of the locals will affirm, there are secret passages leading from that building back into the recesses of the hill. Back in the good old days of Prohibition, liquor stills were hidden there, and those tree chimneys were vents for the distillation process.

Even if this park weren't haunted, it would merit a visit. There are not too many places in the United States boasting the meticulous cement artwork found on these grounds. Still, the place does appear to be most certainly haunted, and you may just catch for yourself a glimpse of the pleasant ghost of McCourtie Park.

27

Spirits among the Spirits

Place Visited: The Lakeside Lounge, a popular tavern and grill located at 11303 E. Chicago Road in the tiny village of Somerset Center, Michigan

Period of Haunting: This haunting spans several decades, with reports from as far back as the 1950s. Much of the activity is recent and ongoing, with the haunting increasing in intensity late in each year.

Date of Investigation: April, 2000

Description of Location: The Lakeside Lounge rests comfortably on the south side of US-12, in the village of Somerset Center, a small population nestled away in the glacial hills of northern Hillsdale County. It is a flat-roofed, single-story, block structure, most of which is actually below street level. The building itself dates back to the late 1920s and has always been a tavern, with the exception of the Prohibition years, during which it served only as a restaurant. Originally, it had two stories, with the basement housing both a watering hole for local inebriates and an office for a gas station. This was back in the days when alcohol and gasoline were served with equal aplomb. The original upper level served as a chalet-style restaurant and was actually quite the place to dine in days of yore. That portion of the building burned down between 20 and 30 years ago and has never been replaced. Situated on what was for years the main route between the downtown areas of Detroit and Chicago, it was not

A tavern for several decades, the building housing
Somerset Center's Lakeside Lounge has hosted
many mobsters in its day as it was located along
the main route between Detroit and Chicago.

uncommon to encounter well-heeled mobsters within
the tavern's walls, as they plied their trade and bick-
ered with bullets over the illegal liquor business. The
Lakeside Lounge is now a community tavern, with live
music for dancing on the weekends and plenty of colorful locals to give the place its fair share of blue-collar
character. It's a friendly place to visit; the drinks are
never watered down, and the hamburgers are among
the largest to be found anywhere. Stop in when you're
thirsty, but make sure your stomach is growling, too, as
all the items on the menu are offered in portions so
generous as to require help in wolfing them down. And
if you wish to kill two birds with one stone, McCourtie
Park, another haunted public site recorded within the
pages of this tome, is just across the road and about
one mile east.

The Haunt Meter: * * * * ½

This establishment, open to the public seven days a week, is one of my favorite haunted places in this book. Taverns are always great places to retreat from the cares of the workaday world, but The Lakeside Lounge not only invites you into its world, it offers you glimpses into the paranormal world as well. Furthermore, witnesses to its ghostly antics abound, from employees past and present, to customers of all ages and persuasions.

Sue Brunty owns and operates The Lakeside Lounge, which she purchased in 1989. A woman of seemingly inexhaustible energy, Sue does just about everything around the tavern, from tending bar to waiting tables to frying up the burgers in the back kitchen. A pleasant and no-nonsense type of lady, Sue is quite open about the haunting of her bar and eatery and was more than happy to relate her experiences to me in between waiting on the customers who kept drifting in and out during my two-hour visit.

One of Sue's first introductions to the lounge's ghostly happenings took place shortly after she bought her new enterprise. She and a former cook named Bill, a retired engineer who helped her out part-time, were alone in the building, getting ready to open up for the day. They were behind the bar, when they heard a female voice wafting through the cooler door next to where they were standing. Having just stocked the cooler with beer, they were well aware there was no one within those chilly confines. "We were stunned for a minute there," relates Sue,

> and just stood there listening to this woman's voice, clear as a bell, coming from inside the cooler. Then Bill just hollered out, "Shut up in there!" and the talking stopped. We opened the door to the cooler, and there wasn't anyone in there. To this day, whenever anyone asks Bill if this place is haunted, he says, "Yeah, there's a broad in the cooler."

Sue purchased the tavern from Rick LeMaster, who

Behind the bar is the water cooler from which a woman's voice sometimes calls out. John Stros, owner of a nearby auto repair shop, has had his own ghostly experiences while helping out at the Lakeside Lounge.

in turn had bought the place after it had burned down under previous ownership. It had been his intention to rebuild the upstairs portion and reopen it as a restaurant. "Rick told me that shortly after he bought the place," says Sue,

> he started to do some renovation work upstairs. It was his plan to rebuild the chalet-style restaurant that was up there. He said he always got a weird feeling while working up there, and felt like he wasn't alone. Then one day when he was up there alone, he heard a loud noise and then all the mirrors on that level just shattered—I think he said there were five of them. They all shattered at the same time. Not long after that, he gave up the notion of renovating the place, and after a while sold it to me. The whole idea of rebuilding a restaurant up there has just been abandoned, and that's why there's only one level now.

Sue purchased the place from Rick in 1989 and

began remodeling work of her own on the remaining level. The services of a young carpenter were retained, and for security purposes during the construction work, he agreed to sleep overnight in the building, making his bed on the pool table, until his work was completed. However, he ended up lasting only two nights in the creepy, old place. "He complained to me about hearing voices all night," says Sue.

> By the end of the second night, he said he couldn't take it any more, that he felt like he was being watched. He heard the voices on the second night, too. The funny part was that, for security reasons, I had locked him in the building and he couldn't get out. After the second night of being scared stiff, I finally had to let him stay nights at my house until his job was finished.

The haunting of The Lakeside Lounge is certainly not exclusive to Sue's tenure. Local legend, which is usually pretty accurate in a small community, holds that the original owner of the place, whose name Sue could not recall, often played host to a colorful array of gangsters who frequented the place during Prohibition. Somerset Center sits quietly alongside what was then the main route between Chicago and Detroit. Rum runners smuggling bottled spirits often stopped in for a bite to eat, and a local old-timer named Jim Kelly recalls that when he was a boy Al Capone used to drop in once in a while. Sue relates:

> Jim is a colorful character around town, he told us that back then the place was called "The Moonlight Chalet," and that it was really a classy place to eat. In fact, the local township offices down the road still have photos of what the place looked like back then, and it really was a high-class place. Anyway, Jim says he was in the restaurant one day in the early 1930s when the door opened and about six nasty-looking men in expensive suits walked in and looked the place over. Then, about a minute later, in walked Al Capone. He

said Capone was really very friendly and nice to everybody there, that they had dinner and then headed on their way.

The original owner may have contributed to the haunting everyone now finds so fascinating. According to Sue and a couple of the regulars in attendance the afternoon of my interview, this gentleman didn't get along very well with his wife. One day, his spouse simply vanished, never to be seen again. Locals still suspect foul play, and for some reason many of them believe she was secretly interred inside the building itself, underneath the area now occupied by the beer cooler, which would explain the woman's voice heard emanating from within. Back in those days, that area of the bar was just a dirt-floor, basement storage area—the perfect place to dig a covert grave.

It is thought that perhaps the ghost of this former owner's wife slips out of the cooler from time to time and glides along on her way through the bar. "When the place still had a restaurant upstairs," says Sue,

> and that was up until close to the time I bought it, the owners would talk about being at the bar and seeing a woman appear near the bandstand. She would stand there a moment and then walk up the stairs leading to the restaurant above. When they would run up there to check the place out, there wouldn't be anyone up there at all, and the doors would still be locked.

John Stros is a local fellow who owns and operates an auto body repair shop across the street from The Lakeside Lounge. Friendly with the owner and most of the patrons, he is well aware of the haunting. He confirmed, without any prompting, the story of the workman who lasted two nights on the pool table before exiting the place for safer refuge. Such unsolicited confirmation adds to my belief that the stories I garner are indeed truthful. John also has stories of his own.

"For a while, I used to work there," says John,

tending the bar and cleaning the place up. Sometimes business would be slow in the afternoon, and that's when I'd really get the creeps. I just knew I wasn't alone in there. It was really creepy. I felt like someone was watching me, and I'd see dark shadows scooting across the room out of the corner of my eye. So I'd play the drums or call somebody to come over so I'd have someone to talk to. There was no way I was ever comfortable when I was alone in there.

A jack-of-all-trades while employed there, John frequently had encounters with the active spirits which still roam around, making themselves at home among the regular, paying guests.

I was over by the bar one afternoon, when I glanced over to the kitchen. There's a cutaway hole in the kitchen wall for the cooks to pass food from the kitchen to the dining area for the waitresses. We had some dishes stacked there, and just as I looked over, they all lifted up off the ledge they were on and flew out into the bar area, smashing all over the floor. This kind of stuff has happened to other people around here, too.

The haunting of this friendly watering hole knows no bounds. Strange things abound in just about every nook and cranny. John continues:

Once, back in 1995, I had to go into the back room, just off the kitchen, to take care of some stock. It was dark in there, and I had some supplies I was carrying. The only light in there is a fluorescent light fixture that you turn on by pulling a string. Well, I kept fumbling around in the dark, trying to find the string with my one free hand, and I couldn't find it. I really started to get ticked off, and a little freaked out, because I'd found that string lots of times before when it was dark in there. It felt like someone was playing games with me. So, I hollered out, "C'mon!" and, when I did, the fluorescent light began to glow, not the whole light, but just a couple of inches of it, just enough of a glow to let me find the string. It was so freaking strange that when I set my stuff down I shut off the light and ran back out into the bar to get one of my friends. I told him he just had to see this for himself, and we went back into the storage area. Again I hollered out "C'mon!" and, sure enough, that bulb began to glow again, just the same couple of inches. It totally freaked us both out and we just ran out of there as fast as we could.

John worked at the bar from about the time Sue bought the place until 1995. Often responsible for tending the bar during the slow hours of the afternoon, he would sit at the bar and watch TV to pass the time.

The bar itself is L-shaped, and there are huge mirrors all behind it. When you sit at the bar you can look in the mirrors and see everything that's going on behind you—you can see the whole barroom reflected in them. I can't tell you how many times I'd be sitting there alone, watching TV, and I'd see the reflection of a dark shadow scooting across the room behind me. I'd look into the mirror and there it would be, shooting across the room. But when I'd spin around to see what was going on, there wouldn't be anyone there. This has happened to a lot of customers, too. Lots of times they'd be sitting at the bar having a cold one, and all of a sudden spin around and look behind them. When they'd ask me about it, I'd just say, "Man, this kind of stuff happens all the time around here."

Apparitional experiences are so commonplace that Sue seems to have become somewhat blasé about it all. Although she admits the place gets a little weird every now and then, she claims she's not frightened by any of the ghostly antics. "I live with it," she says, "so I just ignore it and get used to it. I find it interesting, and I try to figure out what might be causing it all and why, but I don't let it bother me."

As my wife and I sat at a table conversing with Sue about the nature of her haunting, she speculated as to the possible identities of some of the uncorked spirits who have taken up residence in her place of entrepreneurial pursuits.

A former owner told me about a real tragedy that took place around here about 20 years ago. This has always been a popular area for summer vacationers, especially with Lake LeAnn and Lake Somerset so close by. It was a Memorial Day weekend, and two young women stopped in here to wait for their boyfriends. They were supposed to meet here, and then go to the lake together. I'm told they waited a couple of hours or so, and when their boyfriends didn't show, they went out into the parking lot to get in their car to leave. Just as they were approaching their car, a semi-truck came barreling around the curve and went off the road, into the parking lot, and killed them both.

Could this explain the dark shadows so many patrons and employees encounter throughout the bar? Perhaps the girls are still awaiting their errant boy-friends. Who knows?

It's always refreshing and stimulating to encounter such a well-documented haunting, especially when the proprietor has no reservations about citing names of witnesses and dates of experiences. "I had two girls who did work for me in the bar," says Sue.

One was named Pat, and she contracted to do cleaning for me. Well, one Monday she came in to clean the place up, and since we were closed on Mondays back then, I opened the place up and let her in. Since I was worried about security, she agreed that I could lock her in. We didn't want anyone coming in and bothering her while she worked. When I came back several hours later to check on her and see if she had finished, she was petrified. She said that all the while she'd been cleaning up, she thought she could hear distant voices, and that once in a while she would hear something banging around. She said she passed it off as her imagination, but then, after she'd been alone there for a couple hours, she looked out into the lounge area and saw a man walking across the room, from one end of the bar to the other. She said he never looked at her, and she knew right away the guy wasn't real. He just walked across the barroom and disappeared. She refused to be locked in the bar alone after that.

As if this isn't spooky enough, Sue goes on to recount the experience of the other young lady who worked in the bar. Her name is Kathy, and it seems Kathy actually leased the kitchen from Sue at one time.

> Kathy thought it would be a good opportunity for her to make some money, and I thought it would make things easier around here for me. Not long after she started working here, she began to complain about not being alone in the place, that there was someone in there with her. She would come in early by herself, usually around 5 A.M., and start her kitchen prep. She said she'd take her breaks sitting at the bar, and that time and again she'd see the reflection of a man in the mirror as he walked across the room behind her. Then, one morning she was in the kitchen and she turned to see this guy pass right through the kitchen and disappear into the storage area. Our working arrangements went a little sour after that.

Passing shadows, women climbing staircases, and flying dishes ought to be enough to satisfy the cravings of most ghost aficionados, but the haunting of The Lakeside Lounge doesn't seem to stop with the usual paranormal flights of fancy. Sometimes the ghosts get a bit rough with the customers and help.

"I was tending bar one afternoon," remembers Sue,

> and a customer named Belinda was sitting at the bar, watching TV, and chatting with me. All of a sudden she jumped up off her bar stool and looked behind her. When I asked her what was wrong, she said someone had slapped her on the back of the head. I knew she wasn't making this up, because she's not the first one to get slapped by one of our ghosts. One time a young man named Shawn was in the bar with some friends. He was out in the lounge area and walking toward the bar. As he got near the kitchen area he actually stumbled forward, like he lost his balance, and he spun around and looked behind him. He told me someone hit him hard on the back of the head. He was

actually pretty mad at first, but then when he realized there was no one anywhere near him, he thought it was pretty neat that a ghost had slugged him one.

Perhaps the most intriguing incident took place not all that long ago and was witnessed by several people at the same time, including the son of the local sheriff, which I suppose lends some measure of credence to our story. "There were three or four of us," begins Sue,

and we were sitting at one of the tables near the bar, just visiting and passing the time on a slow afternoon. We were the only ones in the bar at the time, and everything was feeling very normal. All of a sudden, a chair from one of the tables behind us just slowly pulled out and turned itself around. Then it scooted right up to our table and tucked itself in next to us, just like someone would do if they were pulling up a chair to join us. It scared the hell out of us. In fact, two of those people got so scared they said they'd never come back, and they haven't—and they're friends of mine.

Although Sue is a reservoir of ghostly information, she is also a regular recipient of paranormal pranks and spectral encounters.

The only time I saw a ghost that wasn't a shadow was when I was tending bar on a slow December day. I went into the ladies' room, and when I looked into the mirror I saw the image of a man looking back at me. He was a middle-aged man, I'd say about 50 or so, with brownish-gray hair that was shaggy and down to his shoulders. I remember he had a beard, and he was wearing an old, dark brown work shirt. The impression I got was that he was from the '30s or the '40s, he definitely wasn't from our time period. I stood there and looked at him for a minute, and then he just vanished.

The Lakeside Lounge is a fascinating public haunt. According to Sue, the strange events continue, although she asserts the activity seems to dramatically escalate during the months of October, November, and December. Some events are quite recent. A young man named J.D. has had the most current encounter with one of the active spirits therein, as he sat watching TV at the bar and noticed the black form of a man pass behind him, its reflection clearly displayed in the mirror before him. And Sue reports consistent cold spots near the kitchen, the least likely place for a drop in temperature, and the appearance of a man passing behind her as she dutifully washed dishes in the back room.

One of the reasons I'm so taken with this story of the macabre is that I keep a home nearby and can frequent the establishment at will, which I fully intend to do. Sue says anyone who wants to belly up to the bar and await a rendezvous with a ghost is more than welcome to do so.

The storage room of the Lakeside Lounge, where the dark form of a ghost is often seen scooting past.

28

Even the Cats See
This Ghost

Place Visited: A sprawling, brick ranch home in Standish, Michigan

Period of Haunting: 1995-present

Date of Investigation: 1998

Description of Location: Standish is a small but thriving community about 25 miles north of Bay City. Heading north from Ann Arbor on US-23, you will find yourself automatically deposited on I-75 North. Continue on approximately another 40 minutes to the Standish exit. The excursion will kill only about an hour or so. If you've a mind, you may also take M-13 north from Bay City and, if you do, be sure to stop off in Pinconning at the H&H Bakery for some terrific cinnamon french toast. But, back to Standish, which is one of the first up-north-feeling towns you'll come to when traveling from the south. The home in question is located about two blocks from the Standish Community Hospital and dates back to 1964. An apartment complex is nearby, which gives the interested reader a hint as to its whereabouts without disclosing its exact location.

The Haunt Meter: * * * * ½

Ed Thayer knew he bought more house than he needed when he purchased this 2,400-square-foot ranch home in the village of Standish. It came with four bedrooms, a spacious kitchen, a huge living room/dining room combination, three baths, and a family room larger than some apartments he had seen. French doors off the family room led to a beautiful deck, from which one could enjoy the lovely view of a flower garden in the far corner of the backyard. Even though a single man didn't need this kind of space, he had fallen in love with the place at first sight, so in he moved with his two best friends, Jasper and Midnight, cats he had raised from the same litter.

Ed first noticed something strange about the house when he discovered there was one bedroom his two feline companions refused to enter. Even if he picked them up and tried to carry them in, they would uncharacteristically claw and nip at him until they earned their freedom. Ed thought this unusual, as the bedroom was painted pink and adorned with pale pink carpeting—hardly the abode of paranormal guests. "Those cats would go anywhere in the house," explains Ed, "except that spare bedroom just off the living room. If you put their food in there and left them alone for a week, I bet they'd starve to death before going in there to eat."

Ed worked an afternoon shift at General Motors in Bay City, about a half-hour's drive south, and would return home most nights around midnight.

> I was having the place redecorated, you know, some new carpet throughout, and I had to do something about that pink bedroom, so after the contractors would leave for the day and I'd get ready for work, I'd put the cats in the family room and close the door so they couldn't get out and mess anything up. I remember one night I came home and right away I noticed that all the doors in the house were closed. The only door I ever kept closed was that family room door so the cats couldn't get out. Well, I went to the family room, opened the door, and no cats. So I started walking through the house, calling the cats and opening doors as I went, and when I got to the master

bedroom and opened that door, there they were, both of them asleep in the middle of my bed. There's no way they could have gotten there on their own—even if they had escaped the family room, I've never known of any cat who took the time to close doors behind him. This would happen quite a few times in the future.

Ed's girlfriend, Holly, lived downstate near Ypsilanti, and sometimes Ed would call her when he got in from work.

Once, I was talking to Holly and the freakiest thing happened. It was well after midnight, and I was drinking a beer while we chatted away about nothing in particular. All of a sudden, Holly says to me, "Ed, I'm getting the strong sensation of someone standing in the family room watching you." It was freaky, because nothing like this has ever happened to Holly before, and besides, she was over 80 miles away. So, I turned around, and from where I was in the kitchen I could see this vague shape of a woman, sort of willowy and light-colored, standing not 15 feet away in the family room, watching me. I described her to Holly and watched her for about five minutes before she sort of faded away. As a sort of validation that I wasn't going crazy, one of the cats, Jasper, had been sitting on the kitchen counter staring at it, too.

How Holly knew Ed had an unannounced visitor that night mystified even her. Later, she had the opportunity to see this woman for herself. "I was up for the weekend to see Ed," says Holly,

and we had been out to Bay City for supper and down to Midland Street for a few drinks. We came back to Ed's place and, after about a half-hour of listening to music and talking, all of a sudden all the lights in the house went out. Now, that wasn't unusual, because in the summer when there's a storm the lights often go out in Standish, and there was a storm booming away outside. We lit a couple of candles and a kerosene lamp and continued to sit on the couch in the family room and watch the lightning split through the night sky.

The entire neighborhood was blacked out. About five minutes later, the lightning flashed really bright, and I could see this woman standing in the far corner of the family room, just watching us. It scared the hell out of me and I screamed. About then, this woman literally flew across the room and into the kitchen and out of sight. Ed saw that part of it, too.

Fascinated by their reclusive houseguest, Ed and Holly decided to break out the Ouija board. With only candles to light their way, it was a spooky atmosphere to say the least. "We quieted ourselves," remembers Ed, "and tried to clear our minds. Then we started working the board. All we got was a date—1923—and a first name—Angela. So, from then on we called the ghost Angela."

If Angela is the name of Ed's ghost, she certainly is watchful. Ed recalls going to bed one night after a grueling shift and falling fast asleep. Sometime around 3 A.M., he says he was awakened by someone pounding on his bedroom door, which he kept closed at night to prevent nocturnal visits from his cats. Jumping up from a sound sleep, he swung open the door, ready to do battle with whomever was there. Immediately, Ed smelled the acrid scent of noxious fumes. Instinctively, he rescued his cats and, with eyes and throat burning, exited the house. It seems the furnace had malfunctioned and had begun to fill the house with toxic gases. Ed credits Angela with pounding out a warning on his bedroom door. "There's no doubt in my mind," says Ed, "that if something hadn't woken me up I'd be dead today."

The haunting of Ed's spacious bachelor's pad continues to this day. He constantly reports doors opening and closing by themselves, and fleeting glimpses of a woman in white sliding through his kitchen. All his efforts to determine the identity of the ghost have been in vain. "I've spoken with neighbors," he says, "but they just don't have a clue as to what's going on. They tell me the former owners never mentioned anything like this, and they lived there for a number of years."

I phoned Ed as I penned this chapter to see if any new twists to the haunting have manifested themselves of late. He insists the home grows more interesting with the passage of time.

> Just last week, I had to run into Bay City to do some shopping. While I was there, a pretty nasty thunderstorm kicked up, and all the way home I was mad at myself for having left my windows open, especially in the family room where my new TV and stereo were. When I got home, all the windows were closed and locked, and although it was pouring down rain outside, there wasn't a single drop on the windowsills. When I tell this story to other people, they tell me I must have shut the windows myself and just forgot about it. But I know that isn't true, because one of the curtains in the family room had been closed in the window, and that's something I would have noticed right away.

I suppose if one must have a ghost in the house, it may as well be a thoughtful ghost.

29

Be Careful What You Play With

Place Visited: A single-story, wood frame home, built in the early 1950s, on Harroun Street in Wayne, Michigan

Period of Haunting: 1993

Date of Investigation: Summer, 1993

Description of Location: Wayne is the westernmost Detroit suburb, a blue-collar town only a few minutes drive east of Ann Arbor. It is home to the Ford Motor Company's Wayne Truck Assembly Plant, a major employer and the factory in which a large share of Ford's trucks are assembled. If headed west on Michigan Avenue as you pass through town, Harroun is a few blocks to the south, just east of Wayne Road. The home discusses is near the Wayne Parks and Recreation Center.

The Haunt Meter: * * * * *

Riley Bennett (no, not his real name) purchased the house on Harroun Street not long after returning home from World War II. He and his wife, Nancy, now deceased, raised two children there and discovered nothing but happiness during their life together in this house.

It wasn't until a couple of years after Nancy's death that Riley began to notice something amiss in his home.

He began to see dark, shadowy figures slide past the doorways of whatever room he happened to be in, sometimes more than one shadow at a time. Accompanying their appearances were loud banging noises emanating from the attic crawlspace above and the distinctly foul odor of decaying trash.

Riley, a man then in his mid-70s, was disturbed and concerned about all this, but not particularly frightened. "I saw too much in World War II to be truly afraid of anything anymore," he says, "but this whole thing was getting a little disturbing to me."

Riley's niece, 22-year-old Natalie, admitted to her uncle that she, too, was upset about all this new activity. "Uncle Riley was pretty OK with it all," explains Natalie, "but this stuff was creepy beyond belief. My bedroom was in the basement, and stuff was happening down there, too. I had lived with Uncle Riley for over a year, and the first few months were fine. But all of a sudden, it seemed like we were being invaded."

Over a period of a few short weeks, the haunting experiences escalated. Riley noticed that his back bedroom and the living room seemed to be the focal points of the disturbance. "It got to where every time I went into either of those rooms, I would see small, dark shadows race across the floor and up one of the walls," he says. "Natalie told me that same thing was happening to her in the basement where her room was, and that some of her friends were getting too scared to come over."

"Sometimes," says Natalie,

I'd have friends over for the evening, and we'd be downstairs just hanging out. Lights would shut off by themselves, and candles we would light would all of a sudden flare up really high. On more than one occasion, we thought we could hear moaning coming from the upstairs of the house. There were times I really didn't feel like coming home from work, and a lot of nights I stayed over at a friend's house.

Riley had heard about my exploits as an amateur paranormal sleuth and invited me over to check things out. I found Riley to be a wonderfully kind man with a very gentle disposition, and a man who still grieved the loss of his wife. After our initial interview, I asked him if I could bring in a friend who seemed to be imbued with psychic proclivities, and he was more than happy to oblige. I made a phone call and, about an hour later, Sharon, a vivacious, young redhead with cheerful blue eyes, knocked on the front door.

Sharon and I stood on the front porch as I filled her in about who lived in the house. I told her nothing about the haunting and, after our conversation, I introduced her to both Riley and Natalie. Again, the conversation took place on the front porch, as Sharon preferred to go into the house without having the occupants inside with her. At no time during any of the initial conversations did anyone get specific about what was happening inside the house; it was simply a time to get to know one another.

Riley and his niece agreed to remain outside on the porch as Sharon and I performed our little walk-through of the premises. Immediately upon entering the living room, Sharon seemed at first stunned and then puzzled. Her eyes narrowed as she gazed intently at one corner of the room. "That's odd," she whispered to herself, "there are little, active shadows racing up the wall in the corner and going through the ceiling." When she asked me if I had seen them, I was more than happy to report that I had not.

Without bothering to examine any more rooms, Sharon went into the kitchen and dragged a chair into the hallway just outside the living room. Standing atop the kitchen chair, she pushed open the trapdoor leading to the attic crawlspace and peered inside, toward the direction of the far corner of the living room. "Oh my God," she said, "there are dozens of them. I've never seen anything like this. They're like small children, only they're not human, and they're all bunched together in the corner. I think this is where they enter and leave the house."

Clearly, Sharon was puzzled and she readily admitted she had never encountered anything like this before. Her sense was that these shadowy figures were less than pleasant, but somewhat frightened of her, if not frightened at all by anyone else. Intrigued, she climbed down off the chair and, giving me a determined look, asked, "Where's Mr. Bennett's bedroom?"

We traversed the hallway to the rear of the home and entered Riley's bedroom. Sharon stood still for a moment, raised her arms about shoulder high, and said, "She's here; I can sense her really strong in this room." Then she began to tell me how Riley's wife was recently deceased, but that she was still a very active presence in that back bedroom, as though she were trying to protect her husband from the entities which had invaded their home. This was all the more convincing to me, considering no one had even mentioned the death of Riley's wife.

As we stood between the bed and the dresser, the entire room slowly and methodically began to darken. Here it was, a beautiful summer's day, without a cloud in the sky, and the entire room was darkening as if someone were pulling the window shades down. "There's a nasty spirit in this house," said Sharon, "and it's here in this room with us now. It wants to attack Riley because of his strong religious beliefs, but his wife won't let it. That's why she's still here—and I know Riley can tell she's very near. He senses his wife's presence quite often."

Well, the darkening room, the description of the home invaders, and a good case of the willies were about to get the best of me, and I wanted to suggest we go back outside and interview Riley and Natalie further. But Sharon would have none of it. Instead, her eyelids narrowed, and it appeared to me she was intently listening to something at a decibel level beyond my ears' perception. Then she said, "He's leaving the room now, his wife won't let him stay." At that, the room slowly began to brighten back to its normal, warm glow.

I've experienced more than my share of paranormal activity, but this was a new one to me. It didn't appear Sharon was talking about your average, run-of-the-mill ghost here. So I was less than pleased when she looked at me with angry eyes and said, "Just what has that girl (referring to Natalie) been doing in this house?" Then she told me to go outside and tell both uncle and niece not to come indoors until we sent for them. I did as told, and, when I returned, Sharon was waiting for me in the living room. "Come on," she directed, "we're going to tear this place apart if we have to, but we're going to find out what she's been up to." With that, she immediately headed for the stairs leading to the basement.

"This is it," proclaimed Sharon, as we stepped into the damp, cool recesses of the basement. This is where it's all taking place." For my part, I still didn't have a clue what she was talking about, but I was willing to go along for the ride. "Start looking," she said, "and let me know if you find anything strange." With that, we began exploring the basement bedroom area, looking under the bed, searching the drawers, and poking our noses into places our proper upbringing normally wouldn't approve of.

We hadn't searched long when Sharon opened a metal footlocker that was tucked away inside a closet and peered inside. "Here it all is," she exclaimed. Inside the footlocker were sundry items pertaining to the black arts—black candles, tarot cards, a role-playing fantasy game, erotic black magic items, and various books on witchcraft.

> They're holding séances and dealing with stuff they know nothing about. They think they're playing games, but this stuff is real. Natalie knows exactly why this stuff is happening in this house. It's gotten out of hand, and she doesn't know what to do about it now.

She thinks she was just playing around, but this isn't any game.

It took a while for Sharon to cool down and, when she did, she went outdoors and took Natalie aside for a "Dutch Uncle" conversation in the neighbor's yard. I couldn't hear what was said, but the intensity on Sharon's face was mirrored by the shame on Natalie's. Afterward, Sharon assured me that Natalie was going to rid the home of anything to do with the black arts.

After a moment's conversation with Riley, Sharon asked permission to go back into the house alone. Riley obliged, Natalie offered no resistance, and at that point I was more than satisfied to wait outdoors. She returned after about half an hour and assured Riley that he would have no further negative feelings about his home. When I asked Sharon what she had done in there, she just said she had done what it takes to clear the house. I pursued the issue no further.

I spoke with Riley a few weeks later just to see if his house still exhibited odd behaviors. He indicated that all was calm and that the house was peaceful. He thanked me for whatever Sharon and I did, and I never let on that it seemed to be his own niece who had brought forth the nastiness and the shadows. A few weeks later, Natalie moved out. Mercifully, the haunting appears to be over.

Index

People and places

Publisher's Credits

Cover Design: Timothy Kocher

Interior Design: Sharon Woodhouse

Layout: Ken Woodhouse and Sharon Woodhouse

Editing: Sharon Woodhouse and Jason Fargo

Proofreading: Sharon Woodhouse, Gabriel Robinson, Karen Formanski, and Ken Woodhouse

Photos: Gerald S. Hunter

Drawing: Tracey Hunter

Index: Sharon Woodhouse

The text of *Haunted Michigan* was set in Bookman Old Style with heads in Zanders.

Notice

Although Thunder Bay Press and the author have exhaustively researched all sources to ensure the accuracy and completeness of the information contained in this book, we assume no responsibility for errors, inaccuracies, omissions, or any inconsistency herein. Special care was taken to preserve respect for the deceased and any slights of people or organizations are unintentional.

Haunted?

If you would like to share your own haunted Michigan experiences with Rev. Hunter, you may contact him by mail at Thunder Bay Press, 1690 W. Brookside Dr., West Branch, MI 48661. We request that you respect Rev. Hunter's privacy and refrain from attempting to reach him at his home or work.

About the Author

Gerald S. Hunter is an ordained United Methodist minister currently serving a parish church in Hartland, Michigan. He was educated at Albion College, where he received a Bachelor of Arts degree in Religious Studies, and at The Methodist Theological School in Ohio, where he received his Masters of Divinity. Rev. Hunter is currently enrolled in the Masters of Counseling program at Central Michigan University in Mount Pleasant.

An avid writer, Rev. Hunter has had articles published in *The Detroit Free Press*, *The Akron Beacon Journal*, and *The Michigan Christian Advocate*. He has also taught creative and business writing at Saginaw Valley State University as an adjunct instructor of English.

Rev. Hunter and his wife, Tracey, maintain a home in Hillsdale County, Michigan.

More Ghost Stories

More Haunted Michigan: New Encounters with Ghosts of the Great Lakes State
by Rev. Gerald S. Hunter
ISBN: 1-933272-01-5, $15.95
More Haunted Michigan brings you antique ghosts from Jackson, theatrical ghosts from Dowagiac, a growling ghost from Mackinac Island, a feline ghost from Otsego, and many more. Join Hunter as he tours the state, documenting the unexplainable and exploring the presence of the paranormal in our lives.

Haunted Michigan 3: The Haunting Continues...
by Rev. Gerald S. Hunter
ISBN: 978-1-933272-37-5, $15.95
Buy a theater ticket, treat yourself to dinner at a nice restaurant, stop in for drinks at the neighborhood tavern, or visit a historical setting. These places and more are yours to visit all across Michigan. Just keep your eyes open and your ears tuned in at all times because the strangers you see and the voices you hear may prove that ghosts are found in places both ordinary and extraordinary.

Michigan Haunts and Hauntings
by Marion Kuclo, "Gundella"
ISBN: 1-978-882376-00-5, $12.95
This collection of Gundella's favorite tales and ghost stories from and about the region—Indian legends, folklore from Michigan's early days as a territory, and modern-day hauntings —is pre-sented with her special blend of story-telling and research.